Hall & Haywood's
Foundation
QUILTS
Building on the Past

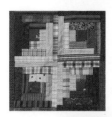

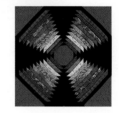

by Jane Hall and Dixie Haywood

American Quilter's Society
P. O. Box 3290 • Paducah, KY 42002-3290

Located in Paducah, Kentucky, the American Quilter's Society (AQS) is dedicated to promoting the accomplishments of today's quilters. Through its publications and events, AQS strives to honor today's quiltmakers and their work and to inspire future creativity and innovation in quiltmaking.

EDITOR: BARBARA SMITH

BOOK DESIGN/ILLUSTRATIONS: ELAINE WILSON

COVER DESIGN: MICHAEL BUCKINGHAM

PHOTOGRAPHY: CHARLES R. LYNCH

Library of Congress Cataloging-in-Publication Data

Hall, Jane   1932-

    Hall and Haywood's foundation quilts: building on the past / Jane Hall and Dixie Haywood

       p.   cm.

Includes bibliographical references.

    ISBN 1-57432-748-8

    1. Patchwork--Patterns   2. Quilting-- Patterns   I. Title: Foundation quilts.   II. Haywood, Dixie.   III. Title.

    TT835 .H33194   2000

    746.46'041--dc21

                         00-009372

Additional copies of this book may be ordered from the American Quilter's Society, PO Box 3290, Paducah, KY 42002-3290 @ $26.95. Add $3.00 for postage and handling.

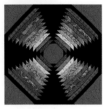

Contents

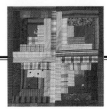

Dedication

We dedicate this book to the quilters of the past on whose work the quilters of the present and the future build.

Acknowledgments

We want to thank students and readers who have passed along their discoveries that have enhanced things we learned in our own work. This knowledge contributes to our ability to share our collective insights with an ever widening audience of enthusiastic foundation piecers.

A special thanks to our quilting friends in the British Isles who have helped us clarify the origins of the Log Cabin pattern in the United Kingdom. Dorothy Osler, Janet Rae, Gill Turley, and Jo Thrussell from the Isle of Man, have given time, thought, and effort to contribute to our understanding of the historic role of this design.

We thank our guest artists who participated in this book, sharing their wonderful quilts and giving you even more extensive projects from which to choose to "taste" the different design categories. And last, but not least, we thank our long-suffering husbands for their continuing support.

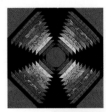
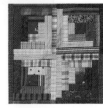

Preface

Our first book, *Perfect Pineapples*, introduced the technique of foundation piecing for a seemingly difficult-to-piece whole-block pattern. The book created, for many people, an awareness of the advantages of working on foundations. However, foundation piecing has a geometric limitation when crossed or inset seams prevent continuing the pressed-piecing process, which is probably why this technique formerly had been used only for whole-block patterns. To solve this problem, in *Precision Pieced Quilts Using the Foundation Method*, we broke ground by dividing blocks into piece-able segments, often combining different foundation techniques. In *Firm Foundations* we developed segmenting into an extended system that allowed the piecing of a wide range of blocks not previously considered for foundation piecing.

Now, in *Foundation Quilts*, we are returning to the original whole-block format of quilts pieced on foundations. Historically, these include string, crazy, Log Cabin, and Pineapple patterns. We are interested in updating these time-honored design categories because we believe we honor the past best by building on it, rather than simply repeating it.

Foundation piecing and its associated techniques have developed over the years, with many people using and developing similar methods, often concurrently. As more quilters worldwide use foundations, we can expect more innovations, applications, and refinements to continue to expand this technique. Foundation piecing is an old-made-new method of working that truly belongs to everyone.

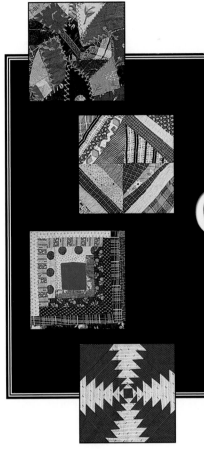

Chapter 1
Overview: The Big Four

This book is based on our belief that in order to make the most of the future, we need to understand and appreciate the past. The four categories of quilts we explore – string-pieced, crazy-pieced, Log Cabin, and Pineapple – were all early foundation-pieced quilts with strong graphic designs achieved with relatively simple construction techniques. These designs have retained their popularity for well over a century. They continue to intrigue and excite quilters with their potential for creative innovation. We expect that to be true for the next century as well.

These categories of quilts were easily adapted to the materials and skill the maker possessed. They were made with a wide variety of fabrics, including various weights and weaves of cotton, silk, and wool, and they were generally worked by hand on a foundation. The stitching ranged from crude to very fine (Photo 1–1).

Photo 1–1

full quilt on page 9

The most common technique used for these patterns was pressed-piecing, colloquially termed "sew and flip" or "flip and sew." This process involves stitching two fabrics together on top of a foundation. Each piece is pressed open onto the foundation after being sewn, before the next piece is added. Quilts were variously tied, embellished, or hand quilted. As sewing machines came into wider use in the latter part of the nineteenth century, machine piecing and even machine quilting became more prevalent (Photo 1–2).

Photo 1–2

full quilt on page 10

Since these early "Big Four" quilts were made from scraps and small strips of assorted weights and types of fabric, often in the same quilt, the foundations provided the needed stability. Foundations were cut to the size needed for the block and were made of whatever fabric was available. These waste fabrics, frequently pieced together from different fabrics, also encompassed a wide variety of materials. Paper foundations, so universally used today, were uncommon for these patterns before the turn of the century. Using paper for foundations came into its own during the '20s

and '30s. Tales are told of the paper being deliberately left in quilts during the Depression era to add warmth.

Foundations have been found in fabric construction as early as the eighth century in Asia. In the Western world, quilts pieced on foundations have been documented in the early nineteenth century in the British Isles and in the latter half of the nineteenth century in the United States. These earliest documented foundation quilts are, surprisingly, Log Cabin designs. This is contrary to our intuition that the simpler string quilts made with scraps would be the forerunners of foundation-based designs (Photo 1–3).

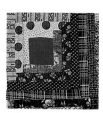

Photo 1–3

full quilt on page 10

The heyday of Log Cabin quilts began in this country in the 1860s and continued until the turn of the century. As people became conversant with the basic pattern, the Pineapple variation emerged relatively quickly. These patterns remain popular to this day (Photo 1–4).

Photo 1–4

full quilt on page 10

It is believed that familiarity with Log Cabin piecing, combined with increased fabric availability for both the design and the foundations, led to creativity and simplification in using "logs," strips, or strings of fabric in other configurations. The seemingly different quilt styles of string and crazy piecing developed toward the end of the period in this way. These two are basically the same type of design, constructed with strips or odd-shaped pieces of fabric. The line between them is fine and, at times, undefinable. Often the colors are placed randomly, creating free-form designs and color collages. At other times, color and placement are planned for a section or for the entire quilt, producing controlled designs. Many times, both string and crazy piecing are used in the same quilt.

Although Log Cabin quilts predated string and crazy quilts, we are proceeding in this book from the simpler designs to the more complex. Each type of quilt is explored in separate chapters, with antique and contemporary examples. There are several projects in each category for you to try. They range from easy to challenging designs suitable for a variety of fabrics. Although our samples were all pieced by machine, these projects can be pieced by hand or machine, depending on your preference and, to some extent, on the foundation material you choose. An additional chapter will provide approaches to quilting to enhance the design of these "back to the future" quilts.

Today, stability continues to be a prime reason for foundation use. But contemporary quiltmakers are using them for additional benefits, prime among them is the precision made possible with updated techniques. Being able to indicate color placement and to register seam alignments directly on the foundations are other advantages that enable intricate or innovative designs to be easily constructed.

Foundations are also important for sewing pieced borders. The elite of "borderdom," pieced borders can be precisely constructed and easily fitted to quilts when made on foundations. Two of our Big Four, string and crazy-pieced designs, are found in a large number of quilt borders, even when there is no string or crazy-piecing in the quilt top.

Log Cabin and Pineapple border patterns make fine frames for quilts, providing linear connections to both the quilt and the adjacent border areas.

Whether you are new to foundation piecing or want to refresh your understanding of the fine points, you will find complete information on materials, marking, fabric cutting, and quilt construction in the Appendix. We urge you to review this section before starting a project.

Photo 1-1. Antique crazy quilt, 60" x 60", dated 1886–1893. Maker unknown. From the collection of Dixie Haywood.

Photo 1–2. (LEFT) Antique string quilt, 66" x 80", circa 1935. Made by Rella Hall Thompson. From the collection of Kathlyn Sullivan.

Photo 1–4. Scrap Pineapple quilt top, 72" x 82", circa 1880. Maker unknown. From the collection of Jane Hall.

Photo 1–3. Sunshine and Shadow Log Cabin spread, 72" x 80", fourth quarter of the nineteenth century. Maker unknown. From the collection of Kathlyn Sullivan.

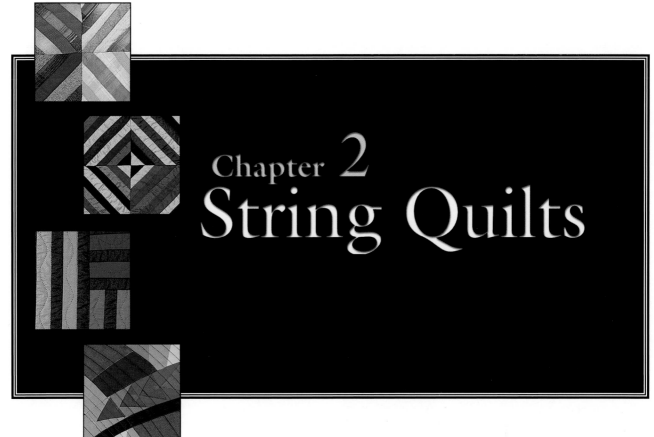

Chapter 2
String Quilts

String and crazy quilts share many characteristics. Both were developed during the last quarter of the nineteenth century. There were several reasons for their appearance at this time. Previously, fabric was expensive and scarce. It had to be made at home, purchased from often far-away mills, or imported. Contrary to the popular image, few scraps were left over from making clothes. Garments of this earlier time were boxy, without much shaping. They were made from rectangles and squares, leaving minimal waste.

After the Civil War, southern communities began building cotton mills as part of the reaction to the devastation of the war and the adjustments of the reconstruction era. There was a wide and popular committment to becoming self-sufficient by using their cotton crops themselves. Labor was cheap and plentiful. As these new mills impacted the established mills of the North, prices dropped and a more abundant supply of affordable fabric was close at hand to many people for the first time.

Concurrently, the expanding industrial revolution generally increased the growth of a middle-class consumer population. Communications improved, fashions changed, and the world was a different place than it had been 20 years earlier. Quiltmaking expanded from being a pastime of a well-to-do leisure class to having a wider influence in ordinary lives.

Making string quilts was a natural way to use scraps of fabric. The popular Log Cabin design had bred familiarity with both the technique of pressed-piecing and the use of foundations for stability. Fabric for foundations was more available. The patterns themselves were simple and non-threatening. With no rigid pattern to follow, pressed-piecing on top of a foundation allowed blocks to be made quickly. These simple blocks could be set together identically or rotated to create a whole much greater than the sum of its parts. When the values were even minimally manipulated or controlled, these designs were highly graphic.

The process of being able to "create" fabric from bits and pieces of different weights, textures, and types of fabric was appealing. Cotton was the most available fabric, but silk and wool were also widely used. Cotton string quilts were often utilitarian, while silk and other fine fabrics furnished Victorian parlors with a variety of string designs.

Making string quilts was also a good way to use wool scraps. Combined with a fabric foundation, wool quilts resulted in warm bedding without the necessity for added batting. Whether the quilts were made from leftover wool scraps, sales-

men's samples, tailor's cuttings, or mill ends, the simplicity of string construction minimized the problems of bulk that more complex patterns presented.

Our first project, TAKE TWO I, page 18, offers two options: a silk wallhanging and a wool lap quilt. They are made with the most basic of string designs, strips laid diagonally across each block. The choice of strip width, value placement, and piecing technique results in two quite different looks and uses.

Betty Caruso used the same diagonal piecing format for her baby quilt, SUNSHINE AND LEMONADE (Photo 2–1). She selected

Photo 2–1

full quilt on page 14

several bright yellows for all the center strips, set in a ground of scrap pastel fabrics, cut in random strip widths. A strong yellow diagonal lattice overlay results when the blocks are joined in rotated groups of four. The quilt is framed with a random piano-key border, a nice counterpoint to the diagonally pieced blocks.

Jane found a wonderful string quilt made with conversation prints at an antique show (Photo 2–2). It is in pristine condition, never having been used or washed, and it dates from the 1890s. The maker used the same

dark wine chintz-type fabric for all the center strips, placing light fabrics on one side of the center strip and dark fabrics on the other. When the blocks are put together, large light and dark on-point squares are formed, reminiscent of a Log Cabin design.

Photo 2–2

full quilt on page 14

In a contemporary use of string-piecing, Barbara Elwell used Thai ikat silks, antique and new, for MEKONG DREAMS (Photo 2–3). She pieced diagonal string blocks, controlling the colors to form a zigzag design which frames the quilt. The center is made from an antique Thai coverlet, repaired and stabilized on one large foundation to keep it the same weight as the outer blocks.

Photo 2–3

full quilt on page 14

Another popular string design involves a vertical arrangement of measured strips. The colors can be random or organized. As the blocks are rotated, diagonal patterns emerge, sometimes subtle and sometimes creating connecting paths across the quilt. Julia Wernicke's quilt has the traditional Rail Fence arrangement with the darkest and the lightest strips in the blocks forming pathways (Photo 2–4). Each block is color-graded from light to dark in rich hues, which creates an incredible glowing depth.

Photo 2–4

full quilt on page 15

Dixie's WALTON MOUND project, page 28, is a contemporary measured-string design pieced on large rectangular foundations. The color arrangement and the angularity of the design re-interpret a Native American motif.

String quilters have quickly branched out to using foundations in shapes other than square blocks. Jane's turn-of-the-century Spider Web wool quilt top contains blocks made with eight string-pieced wedges (Photo 2–5). The strips, cut in random widths, are somewhat muted, except for a bright pink that forms windmills at the block centers and is repeated sporadically in the wedges. The octagonal blocks are set together with plain squares which have been basted onto foundation fabric to make them the same weight as the wedges, forming a Kaleidoscope-like pattern.

Photo 2–5

full quilt on page 15

During the first part of the twentieth century, particularly in the hard times of the '30s, string designs proliferated. Quiltmakers used both fabric and newspaper foundations to literally make something from nothing. Stars of various configurations were especially popular. Photo 2–6 shows both sides of a star pattern, so you can see the foundation.

Photo 2–6

full block on page 15

Agnes Adkison inherited a 1920 family quilt called STAR EVERLASTING, made with kite-shaped segments in muted fabrics (Photo 2–7). The segments were machine pieced on catalog page foundations. They were joined into four-pointed stars, which were set together with elongated red diamonds. The resulting graphic red windmills appear to float on a background of soft string piecing.

Photo 2–7

full quilt on page 16

CHRISTMAS STARS, made by Eileen Sullivan, an innovative contemporary quiltmaker, is a dynamic six-pointed star design made with string piecing on freezer paper (Photo 2–8). The star points, of green and black strips, appear three-dimensional and woven as they seem to spin on the background of red and black strips.

Photo 2–8

full quilt on page 16

Sharon Norbutus has taken string piecing to a new dimension in GLOBAL WARMING, by using what she calls "bent-bias" piecing (Photo 2–9). With a

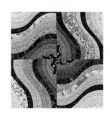

Photo 2–9

full quilt on page 16

background in textiles and clothing and an interest in the uses of bias, she was inspired by June Ryker's curved log designs. Working on foundations is essential to keep the curves and reverse curves flat. Her technique is, as she says, "dangerous, boring, and tedious, but exciting" because she "doesn't know what will happen next" when she is working.

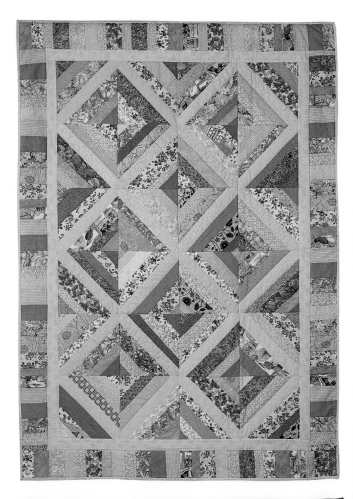

Photo 2–1. (TOP LEFT) SUNSHINE AND LEMONADE, 58" x 42", 1998. Made by Betty Caruso.

Photo 2–2. (BOTTOM LEFT) Conversation-print string quilt, 75" x 82", circa 1895. Maker unknown. From the collection of Jane Hall.

Photo 2–3. (ABOVE) MEKONG DREAMS, 76" x 111", 1999. Thai silk ikat string quilt, antique segments and fabrics, restored and constructed by Barbara R. Elwell.

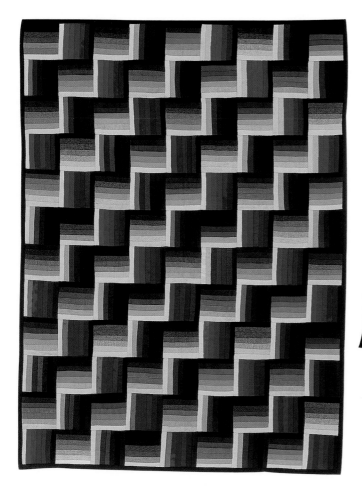

Photo 2–4. (LEFT) Wool Rail Fence quilt, 51" x 67", circa 1900. Maker unknown. From the collection of Julia S. Wernicke.

Photo 2–5. (RIGHT) Wool Spider Web top, 63" x 64", circa 1900. Maker unknown. From the collection of Jane Hall.

Photo 2–6. Eight-pointed star blocks, front and back views, circa 1930. Maker unknown. Note the comic strip foundations. From the collection of Jane Hall.

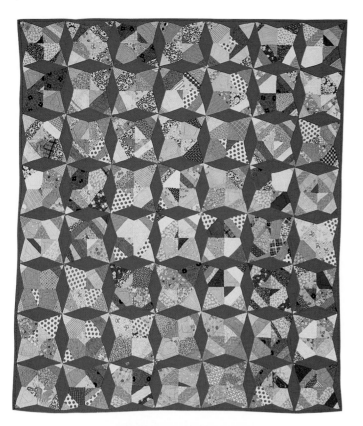

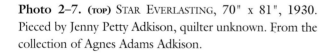

Photo 2–7. (TOP) STAR EVERLASTING, 70" x 81", 1930. Pieced by Jenny Petty Adkison, quilter unknown. From the collection of Agnes Adams Adkison.

Photo 2–8. (BOTTOM) CHRISTMAS STAR, 35" x 34", 1996. Made by Eileen Sullivan.

Photo 2–9. (TOP) GLOBAL WARMING, 48" x 56", 1994. Made by Sharon Norbutus.

Photo 2–10a. (BOTTOM) BORDEAUX STAR, 75" x 45", 1996. Made by Jane Hall.

Caryl Bryer Fallert, one of the most innovative quiltmakers of this century, works almost entirely on foundations and uses string quilting extensively and creatively. Her FLYING GEESE AND RAINBOWS, a contemporary string project with graceful curves, on page 32, is constructed with brilliant colors and two different string-piecing techniques.

Quilters are not only using string piecing for parts of a design, but also using it effectively as a background, creating a texture and interest that a single piece of fabric cannot convey. Jane's BORDEAUX STAR combines string and crazy piecing to create the wedges between the Mariner's Compass points (Photos 2–10a and b). By positioning the strips in each wedge at the same angles, even though randomly, a curved effect is created.

The versatility of string piecing for borders, with strips sewn straight or at an angle, measured or cut randomly, makes it suitable for any type of quilt. String borders also preclude any one

Photo 2–10b. (DETAIL) BORDEAUX STAR.

fabric dominating or competing with the focus of the quilt.

Contemporary quilters, working with yardage rather than scraps, are also using string piecing for the controlled strip-piecing concept created by Barbara Johannah in the 1970s. The technique of stitching long strips of fabric together and cutting across the "strip-set" creates already sewn together shapes which are then resewn to create designs. With the advent of rotary cutting, the process became even speedier and more popular.

Too often, however, the long seam lines are sewn slightly unevenly, causing wobbly strips and problems when joining the stitched segments or "slices." In addition, the multiple pieces and seams of the strip-set, and the slices made from it, can easily become stretched and distorted. On the other hand, in a strip-set sewn on the lines of a marked foundation, the strip width will be precise, the segment shapes exact, and the joining points will have no unexpected variations.

String Quilting Projects

String piecing, long considered mundane, is in fact a varied, versatile, and ever-evolving technique. The following hands-on projects will introduce you to a variety of types of string designs, traditional and innovative, controlled and free-form. Use them to sample this easy-flowing way of working and then make the technique a part of your

quilting repertoire. To familiarize yourself with the basics of string piecing, we suggest you turn to the "How to Press-Piece" section of the Appendix, page 145, and make the three sample string blocks there. They each illustrate a different pressed-piecing technique, all of which are commonly used in string piecing.

Select an appropriate foundation. For techniques with controlled designs, it will be necessary to mark the foundations. (See the Appendix, pages 147–150, for a description of types of foundations and marking options.) Determine whether the foundation will be the size of a finished block or whether it will have a built-in seam allowance. We often use a finished-size foundation when string piecing on temporary foundations because it can be difficult to pull small bits of foundation out of the seam allowances. Again, the type of project and the fabric used to make it will influence this choice. All of the projects were constructed with a sewing machine, but they can be adapted for handwork.

We begin with one basic string design made with two different materials, resulting in two completely different projects. The diagonal string block is one of the most uncomplicated blocks. Made with either scraps or controlled colors, it is simple enough for a beginner, but it has enough graphic possibilities for the most sophisticated quilter.

Take Two I

Photo 2–11. TAKE TWO I, 48" x 48". Made by Dixie Haywood.

The placement of values in this wool lap quilt, with simple diagonal string piecing, adds punch to the secondary designs created by the piecing. It is desirable to use batting as a foundation to provide loft and texture for the wool piecing, but with only batting as a foundation, the block will be difficult to control. Paper is added for stability, and the combination with the batting forms an unusual foundation with both temporary and permanent elements. Use cotton batting because the heat and steam needed to press the wool will melt polyester.

TECHNIQUE:
Random Top Pressed-Piecing

SIZE:
48" x 48"

BLOCKS:
Thirty-six 8" (finished) blocks

MATERIALS:
Assorted selection of wool scraps or remnants, approximately 2 yards total

Wool for backing – 1 yard or large scraps, preferably with a hard finish

Typing paper and cotton batting for foundations

Cable cord – 6 yards of #9/32

Optional – 6 yards ¼" width twill tape

Usual sewing supplies

Construction

1. Cut thirty-six 8" squares of paper and cotton batting. Baste a paper square to each batting square. The paper stabilizes the stretchy batting without adding permanent weight.

    Option: Use a permanent block foundation of cotton flannel, cut 8½" square, and eliminate batting altogether.

2. Cut wool fabrics into strings, ranging from 1¼" to 1¾" wide, saving larger scraps for corner pieces. Do not cut pieces any narrower; wool seam allowances are bulky.

3. Divide the fabrics into light and dark piles. Have no fabric in the dark pile that is lighter than the darkest fabric in the light pile.

4. Following the basic instructions in the Appendix for Random Top Pressed-Piecing, page 145, start piecing in the center of the block, adding strips and stitching on the batting side of the foundation. Sew a total of nine strips. Most of the blocks, but not all, are constructed with the same fabric added on both sides of the center strip. Piece 12 light blocks and 24 dark blocks. You will want to have enough contrast in pattern or color between adjacent strips so that one does not fade into the next. Extend all the strips beyond the foundation, trimming them with a ¼" seam allowance when the block is complete. Press firmly. Wool requires steam to lie flat.

    Staystitch each block outside the edge of the foundation, in the seam allowance, with a short stitch, using the edge of the foundation as a guide.

5. Lay out four dark blocks for the middle, with the center strips creating a square on point. Add a row of light blocks around the dark squares, arranging them so their center strips form an X where they join the inside blocks. Finish with a border of dark blocks, forming squares on point where they meet the light blocks (Fig. 2–1, quilt layout, page 20). Double check before you sew the blocks together. It's easy to mix up the alignment! Join the blocks.

6. Carefully remove the temporary paper foundations, trying not to stretch the edges of the wool. To further stabilize the edge of the quilt, which is all bias, cut four pieces of twill tape the length of a side and stitch the tape in the seam allowance on the wrong side of each edge of the quilt.

7. Cut 6 yards of bias strips that are 1¾" wide. For best results, you will want to use a lightweight wool. Cover the cable cord and stitch it around the quilt ¼" from the edge, joining it near, but not at, a corner.

8. Cut, and piece if necessary, a 52" backing. Layer the quilt top and backing, right sides together, stretching the backing taut. Pin on all sides.

9. Using the stitching line for the cord as a guide, sew the layers together around the outside edge. Leave an opening along the center of one side. Turn the quilt right side out, close the opening by hand or machine, and press the quilt lightly. Lay the quilt flat and pin the layers together.

10. The quilt was machine quilted in the ditch to give the look of a comforter. You could also tie it from the back or quilt it with a large stitch and heavy thread, by hand or machine. A fine quilt stitch would vanish into the wool.

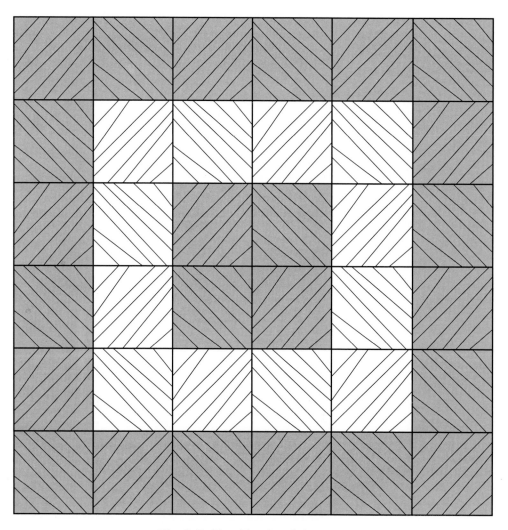

Fig. 2–1. TAKE TWO I quilt layout.

Take Two II

Photo 2–12. TAKE TWO II, 28" x 28". Made by Jane Hall.

This basic string design is a wallhanging made with bright silk fabrics. The measured strings of rich colors are placed on the diagonal of each foundation, creating diamond designs when the blocks are rotated and sewn together. One color was used as a frame for the outer border, with pieces of it also placed within the body of the quilt. The lightweight foundations could be removed but were left in as permanent supports to avoid stressing the silk.

TECHNIQUE:
Under Pressed-Piecing

SIZE:
28" x 28"

BLOCKS:
Thirty-six 4" (finished) blocks

BORDERS:
⅜" (finished) inner black border
2" (finished) outer green silk
  border

MATERIALS:
Assorted silk fabrics, scraps,
  and remnants, approximately
  2 yards total of varying colors. Be sure to have some
  black and neutral shades to
  mix with bright colors.

½ yard of one silk for borders
  and to use in body of quilt

Stabilizer for borders (see note)

1 yard black cotton print for
  backing and binding

Lightweight interfacing foundations cut into thirty-six 4½"
  squares

Cotton batting

Usual sewing supplies

NOTE: Some silks are more fragile than others, and silk frays easily when handled. It may be necessary to iron on a light-weight fusible stabilizer before cutting the fabric into strips. Choose one that provides stability without appreciably changing the hand of the fabric.

Since most of the silks used in the sample were dupioni weight, the strips were not fused before being stitched to the foundations, although it might have made them easier to handle both for positioning and stitching. It was essential to fuse the border strips to stabilize the fabric and match the weight of the borders to that of the body of the quilt. Using a cotton backing made the quilt firmer and easier to control during the quilting.

Construction

1. Cut silk into strips an ample 1¼" wide. Working with silk requires a slightly wider seam allowance (up to ⅜") to counteract the fraying and spring of the fabric. The center and corner strips will finish wider than the others. If you are working with scraps, the longest must reach from corner to corner diagonally across the foundation, with an adequate seam allowance on each end.

2. Because this is a controlled design with the diagonal strips matched as the blocks are joined, the foundations must be marked with seam lines. Trace the block pattern (page 23) on each foundation, marking all the sewing lines. Because of the bias edges on the outside of each block and the type of fabric, Jane used foundations with the seam allowance added to stabilize the outer edges.

3. Cover the foundation with strings, following the general under pressed-piecing directions in the Appendix, page 147. Take special care to press each strip firmly to the foundation after it is sewn, to avoid pleats and bubbles in the slippery fabric.

For this design, five colors were used in each block. Each color was repeated on each side of the center diagonal strip, for a total of nine strips. Select varied colors and values within the blocks for contrast.

4. After the final strips are sewn on each block, press the block firmly from both sides and trim any excess fabric at the edge of the foundation, leaving a ¼" seam allowance beyond the foundation. Stay-stitch the outside edges all around the block with a small stitch in the seam allowance.

5. Arrange the blocks on a design wall or table, keeping the colors and values spread evenly over the face of the quilt. Stitch the blocks together, matching the seams (Fig. 2–2, quilt layout).

6. Border the quilt with a narrow black inner border. True the edges. Add the outer border, butting the corners.

7. Layer, baste, and quilt by machine. Quilt in the ditch to emphasize design areas, such as the center diagonal strips and the squares on point where the corners of four blocks meet, and around each border. Bind the raw edges in black cotton.

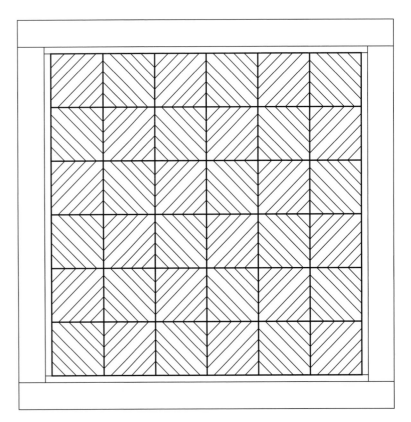

Fig. 2–2. Take Two II quilt layout.

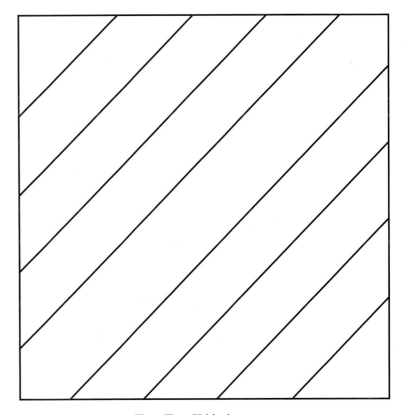

Take Two II block pattern.

Strip-Set Play

Photo 2–13a–d. These are samples of some of the quilt patterns that can be made with foundations. Rail Fence (a), Nine Patch (b), Mock Log Cabin (c), End of the Day (d).

Use under pressed-piecing and marked freezer paper foundations to play with the process of strip piecing on foundations. We show several designs in Photo 2–13, page 24, that are well-adapted to foundation use. You can consider other designs for this method, such as the Lone Star made with strips cut on an angle, eight-pointed stars pieced with diamonds, and the enormous variety of Op Art designs, which depend for their graphics on absolute accuracy at the points where the values contrast.

FREEZER PAPER is a good choice for strip piecing on foundations because it will hold each strip firmly in place as it is sewn and pressed. Both ¼" printed grids and ordinary freezer paper were used for the samples. All the steps were sewn by machine.

Designs with Measured Strips (such as Rail Fence and Nine Patch)

1. Prepare the foundation by drawing sewing lines on the dull side of a piece of freezer paper that has been cut to match strips of fabric cut across the width of the yardage.

Photo 2–13a

full quilt on page 24

The Rail Fence sample requires a strip-set containing four 1" finished strips, which will be cut into 4½" squares, to make 4" finished squares. You will need 16 squares to make the sample (Fig. 2–3).

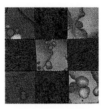

Photo 2–13b

full quilt on page 24

The Nine-Patch sample is made from two different strip-sets, each containing three 1" finished strips. One strip-set will have dark-light-dark values, and the other will have light-dark-light values. Cut the strip-sets apart as indicated in

Fig. 2–4, at 1½" intervals, and combine them to make 3" finished squares. To make the sample shown, you will need 13 Nine-Patch blocks and 12 plain squares cut 3½".

Mark the colors on the Rail Fence and Nine-Patch foundations to avoid confusion. Cut fabric strips with an ample ¼" seam allowance on all sides.

2. To lessen the chance of the iron touching the shiny side of the freezer paper, which would deposit wax on the iron, lay the first strip of fabric on the ironing board, wrong side up. Position the freezer paper over it, shiny side down, making sure the drawn area is covered with fabric that extends at least ¼" over the lines on all sides. Press the paper on the fabric lightly. Try not to iron the paper to the ironing board.

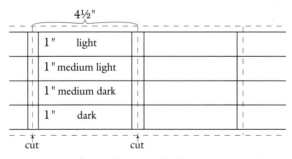

Fig. 2–3. Making strip-set for Rail Fence. Solid lines are sewing lines, dashed lines are cutting lines.

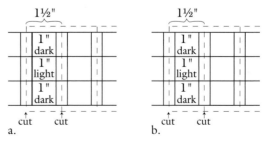

Fig. 2–4. Making strip-set for Nine Patch. Solid lines are sewing lines, dashed lines are cutting lines.

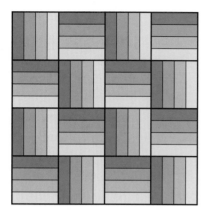

Fig. 2–5. Rail Fence assembly.

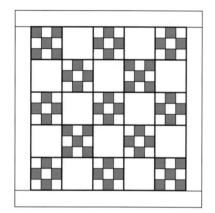

Fig. 2–6. Nine-Patch assembly.

3. Cover the foundations with strips, using under pressed-piecing (see Appendix, page 147). Pin along the strips as you position them to hold them in place. After opening the sewn fabric strips, the long cut edge of each one should cover the next stitching line with an adequate seam allowance. If it overlaps the line by more than ¼", fold back the foundation on the next sewing line and trim the seam allowance to ¼".

4. When the final strip has been added, press the strip-set firmly, first from the fabric side, then from the paper side to anchor all the edges.

5. Cut the strip-sets apart, remembering to add ¼" seam allowances at each cut (4½" cuts for Rail Fence, 1½" for Nine-Patch). Assemble the pieces following the design layouts, pinning points and seam lines. Sew the blocks together to complete the sample. (See Fig. 2–5 for Rail Fence assembly and Fig. 2–6 for Nine-Patch assembly.) Hold the pieces steady as you stitch because freezer paper tends to slip against the feed dogs.

6. Leave the freezer paper in place until the project has been completed but remove it from the seam allowances to reduce bulk. Press the seam allowances open to retain the accurate points and the seam intersections.

Designs with Geometric Shapes (such as Mock Log Cabin and End of the Day)

Many patterns contain identical shapes, such as triangles, diamonds, and trapezoids, and these can be constructed easily and efficiently by cutting them from a strip-set. Follow the basic strip-set directions for designs with measured strips (page 25), but at Step 5, cut shapes rather than strips from the strip-set. Shapes can be drawn onto the prepared foundations before or after the strips are sewn.

Photo 2–13c

detail

full quilt on page 24

For the Mock Log Cabin quilt sample, the block is constructed of triangles cut with their long sides parallel to the strips. (The sample, shown on page 24, is made with six 1" strips of graduated colors. Sixteen triangles were used to make the four blocks.) Mark strip seam lines and triangles on the dull side of a piece of freezer paper (Fig.

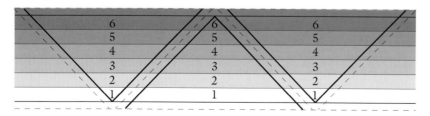

Fig. 2–7. Set-strip foundation for Mock Log Cabin, with segments marked for cutting.

2–7). A triangular ruler is helpful for marking the foundation, dovetailing the shapes. Make sure the legs of the triangles are equal in length, and leave 1" between each triangle to allow for the angled seam allowances.

Piece the strip-set following the basic strip-set directions for designs with measured strips (page 25).

Cut out the triangles, allowing for a ¼" seam allowance on all sides. Stitch them together in like pairs to make half-blocks. To make a block, join a light half to a dark half. Rotate the blocks to form a Log Cabin-type design against a reverse color background. Sew the blocks together to complete the sample (Fig. 2–8).

Photo 2–13d

detail

full quilt on page 24

For the End of the Day quilt sample, after preparing the foundation with sewing lines, trace 16 triangle shapes on the foundation, as shown in Fig. 2–9, positioned with their long sides perpendicular to the strips. Piece the strip-set with six 2" strips of alternating colors. Making sure to allow a ¼" seam allowance on all sides, cut out the triangles and join them to make four 8" pinwheel blocks. Sew the blocks together to complete the sample (Fig. 2–10).

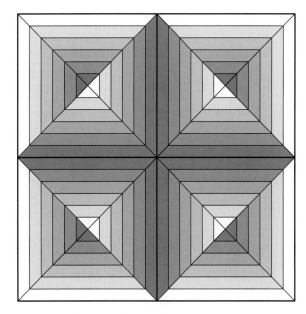

Fig. 2–8. Mock Log Cabin sample assembly.

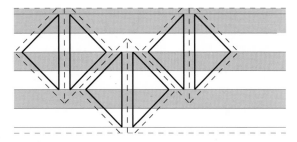

Fig. 2–9. End of the Day strip-set with segments marked for cutting. Solid lines are sewing lines, dashed lines are cutting lines.

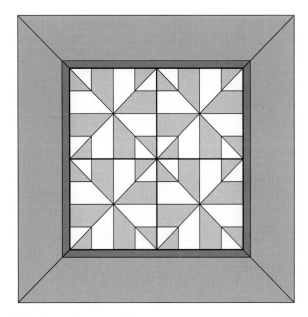

Fig. 2–10. End of the Day assembly.

Walton Mound

Photo 2–14. WALTON MOUND, 32" x 41". Made by Dixie Haywood.

This strip quilt was inspired by a Native American design seen at the Indian Temple Mound Museum in Fort Walton, Florida. Use as many shades of each color as you can for the best effect. Graphed freezer paper was used as a foundation to make accurate marking easy.

Photo 2–14

detail

full quilt on page 28

TECHNIQUE:
Under Pressed-Piecing

SIZE:
32" x 41"

BLOCKS:
Three different sizes of rectangular blocks (see Quilt Assembly diagram, page 30.)

BORDERS:
3" (finished) outer border
1" (finished) middle border
2" (finished) inner border

MATERIALS:

Fabric	Shade	Yards each
Brown	1	2½
Rose	1 to 3	⅛
Green	1 to 3	⅛
Gold	1 to 4	¼
Teal	1 to 4	¼
Red	1 to 6	¼

Backing – 1¼ yards

Foundations – printed grid or freezer paper with lines drawn on each section

Batting

Usual sewing supplies

Cutting Directions

A ⅜" seam allowance is added to each end of the strips. Strip widths have ¼" seam allowances; cut them amply and accurately for easiest piecing.

Fabric	Size	Number
Rose	1½" x 8½"	3

In addition, cut and piece shades to form a strip 1½" x 47" for the middle border.

Teal	1½" x 10¼"	6

In addition, cut and piece shades to form a strip 1½" x 47" for the middle border.

Green	1½" x 5¼	3
	1½" x 14	3
Gold	1½" x 10½"	4
Red	1½" x 5¼"	3
	1½" x 13¾"	3
	1½" x 15½"	5

Brown

Solid fabric can appear to change color depending on how it is positioned. To prevent color change, cut the strips and borders on either the lengthwise-grain (warp) or cross-grain (weft), depending on their placement within the quilt. Mark the grain line of each strip after cutting to avoid confusion. For the most efficient fabric use, cut the borders and the longest pieces first.

		Grain	
		Across	Down
Strips			
	1¼" x 5¼"	3	3
	1¼" x 8½"	2	
	1¼" x 10¼"	5	
	1¼" x 10½"		7
	1¼" x 13¾"	3	
	1¼" x 14"		2
	1¼" x 15½"	5	
	1¼" x 19¼"		1
	1¼" x 20¾"	1	
Borders			
	3½" x 32½"	2	
	3½" x 41½"		2
	2½" x 24½"	2	
	2½" x 33½"		2
	1½" x 9½"	2	2

Binding

2" wide

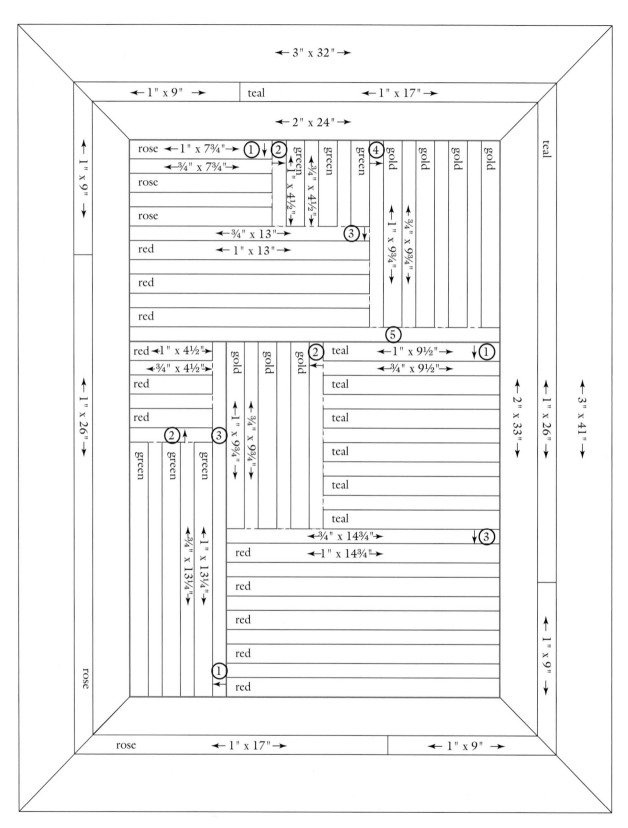

Figure 2–11. Quilt assembly. Draw WALTON MOUND on a foundation.

Construction

1. Following Fig. 2–11, page 30, draw the quilt, without borders, on a purchased grid paper or freezer paper. Under pressed-piecing will reverse the design in a mirror image, so it will look like the photo when finished. To avoid confusion, mark the strip colors on the foundation as you go.

2. Cut the foundation in three sections, indicated by the red lines on the layout. The piecing order is numbered and includes all the color and background strips in that section.

3. Press the first piece right side up on the shiny side of the freezer paper, covering the first drawn lines and having a ¼" seam allowance that extends beyond the foundation. After each strip has been sewn, fold the foundation back on the next stitching line and trim the fabric leaving a ¼" seam allowance. When the sections have been completed, sew them together and add the inner border, mitering the corners.

4. For the middle border, sew the 9½" brown strips to each end of the rose and teal pieced strips. Cut each of these border pieces apart within the colored section to form a 28" and a 37"

border of each color with the brown fabric at the ends. Stitch to the inner border, following Fig. 2–11, mitering the corners. Add the final borders; miter the corners.

5. Remove the foundations, layer, baste, and quilt. Bind with brown. This quilt was hand quilted in the ditch on all seams, with wavy lines down the center of each colored strip, including those in the border. The border was quilted with parallel diagonal lines extending across all three brown borders, changing direction in the center of each side.

Flying Geese and Rainbows

Photo 2–15. FLYING GEESE AND RAINBOWS, 25" x 25". Made by Caryl Bryer Fallert.

Use your string-piecing skills to create this contemporary Flying Geese quilt design with award-winning quiltmaker Caryl Bryer Fallert's trademark Flying Geese. Several techniques, as well as curved piecing, make this a challenging project. The fabrics are Caryl's own shaded, hand-dyed cottons. See Resources on page 158 for more information about these or use the color key on page 34 to assemble fabrics of your choice for this project.

TECHNIQUES:
Under Pressed-Piecing, Random Top Pressed-Piecing, Conventional Piecing

SIZE:
25" x 25"

BLOCKS:
Six patterns, joined to make a 21" square

BORDERS:
2" (finished) black borders

MATERIALS:
One fat-eighth yard fabric packet for each color gradation:

Brilliant greens (color key G1–G8)
Rainbow oranges (color key O1–O8)
Brilliant purples (color key P1–P8)
Light gray to black (color key Gr1–Gr8)

¾ yard solid black for borders, backing, and sleeve

¼ yard solid red, cut across fabric width, for binding

Batting

Thread – medium gray, black, red, medium blue

Freezer paper for foundations

Usual sewing supplies

Cutting Directions

Using the color key, mark the color numbers on each fabric to avoid mistaking similar colors (Fig. 2–12, page 34).

Cut the strips of graduated fabric on the lengthwise grain. (Strips will be 18" long.)

The 1½" strips will be used for random top press-piecing the *b* templates.

The wider strips will be used for under press-piecing the *a* templates.

Brilliant Green Packet
two 1½" strips of each color
one 2" strip of each color

Rainbow Orange Packet
two 1½" strips of each color
one 2" strip of O1
one 3½" strip of O2
one 3" strip of O3, O4, and O5
one 2½" strip of O6, and O7

Brilliant Purple Packet
two 1½" strips of each color
one 2¼" strip of each color

Light Gray to Black Packet
These fabrics will be used for the *c* templates and should not be cut into strips. Be especially careful when cutting Gray #6 (Gr6) because you will have just enough if you are using fat eighths.

Solid Black
Cut fabric vertically into four 2½" strips for the border, one 6" strip for the casing, and use the remainder for the backing.

Solid Red
Cut four 2" x 26" strips for binding.

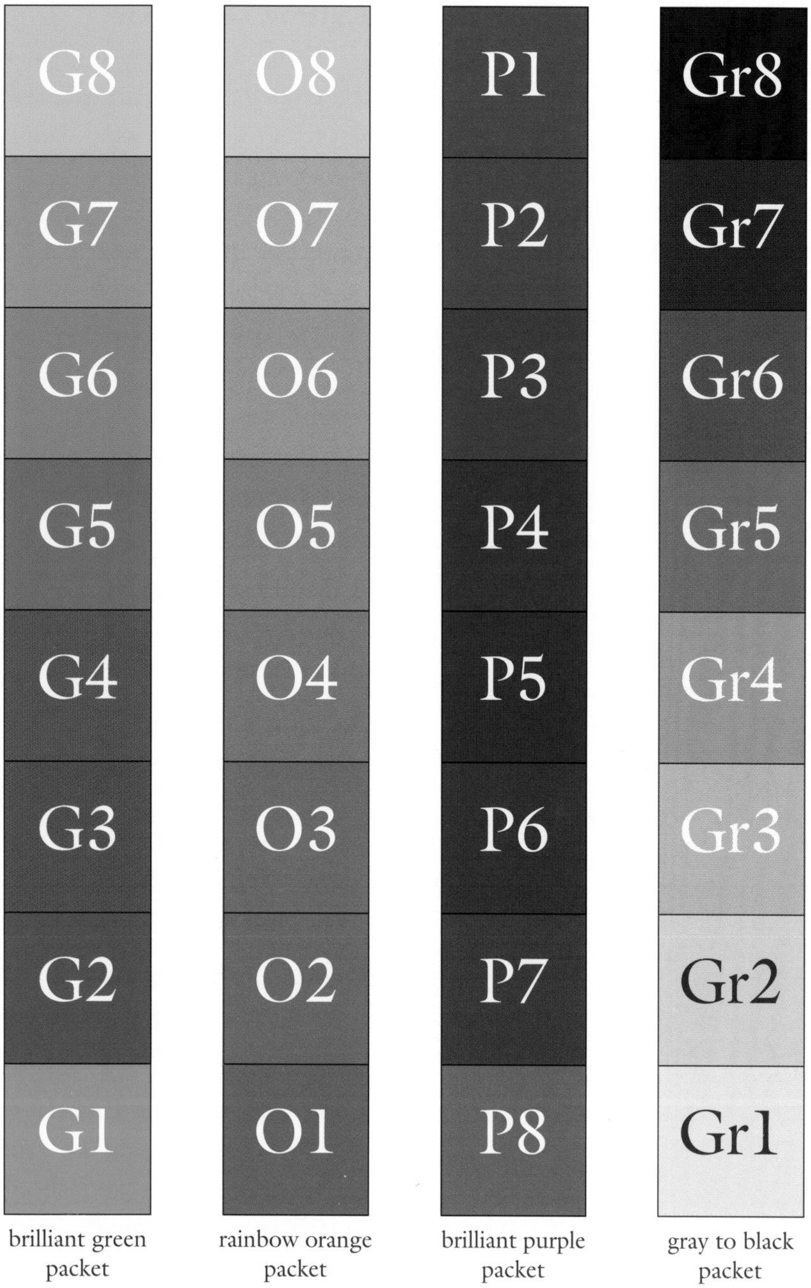
G8
G7
G6
G5
G4
G3
G2
G1
brilliant green packet
O8
O7
O6
O5
O4
O3
O2
O1
rainbow orange packet
P1
P2
P3
P4
P5
P6
P7
P8
brilliant purple packet
Gr8
Gr7
Gr6
Gr5
Gr4
Gr3
Gr2
Gr1
gray to black packet

Fig. 2–12. Color key. Use this key to purchase or dye fabrics.

Construction

1. Trace the six sections of the pattern (pages 40–45), including the registration marks across the seam lines. Enlarge each section to 135% at a drafting or photocopy shop that has large-format copiers.
2. To make a master pattern, tape the sections of the enlarged copies together so that all the lines match at the edges, butting the outer edges for a smooth seam. Do not overlap the patterns. Make any adjustments necessary so the lines of the pattern flow smoothly from one section to the next. You should have a 21" x 21" drawing of the quilt design, in a mirror image of the photograph of the quilt.
3. Code all the pieces, marking the kind of template (a, b, or c) and the piecing order number on each one. (See piecing codes diagram, Fig. 2–13 on page 35.)
4. Tape or press the edges of two pieces of freezer paper together to make a sheet large enough to retrace the pattern. Trace on the dull side with a fine-point permanent marker, which will allow you to see the design on both sides of the paper. Transfer the piecing codes from the master pattern to the freezer paper. In addition, write the color on each template, following the color placement diagram (Fig. 2–14, page 36). To avoid confusing the sets of numbers, use a

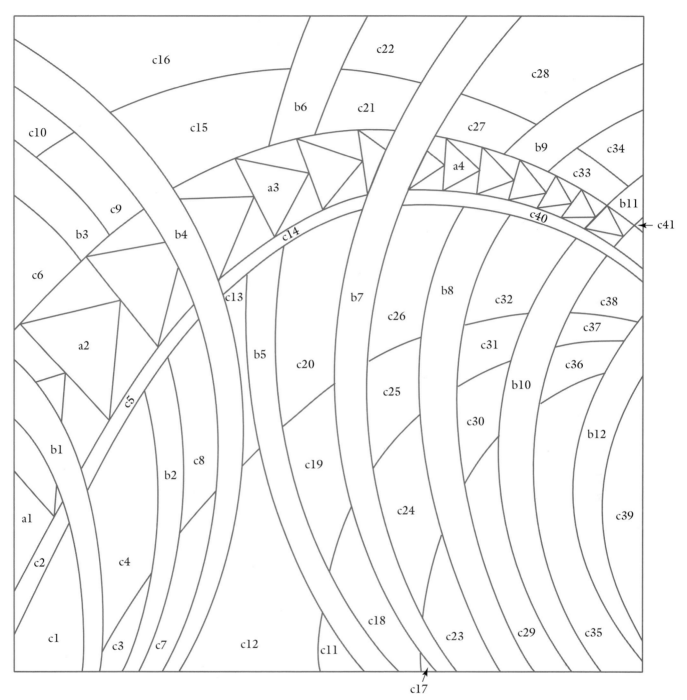

Fig. 2–13. Piecing codes.

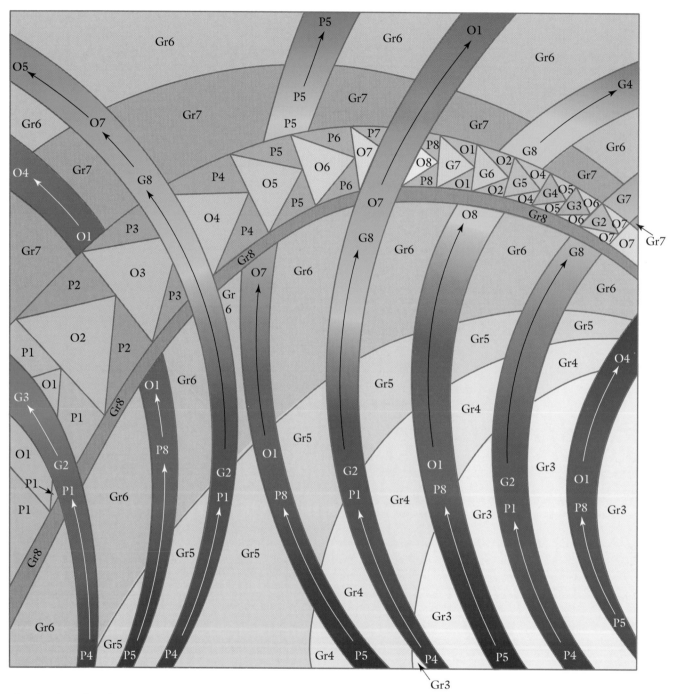

Fig. 2–14. Color placement.

different color for the piecing order and the colors. Be sure to draw the registration marks. They are needed to match the templates when you are assembling the quilt.

5. Cut the freezer paper apart for the foundation templates. There are four *a* templates, made of sections of pieced flying geese in marked colors. The 12 long, thin *b* templates are constructed with shaded colors, and the 41 *c* shapes are individual pieces, all in shades of gray. As you cut them out, place them on the appropriate part of the master pattern to avoid confusion.

6. Piece the four *a* templates by using under pressed-piecing (see Appendix, page 147) with the shiny side of the freezer paper down. Using the wide strips, begin piecing at

the bases of the triangles, working up to the other edge. Caryl suggests using a very short stitch (15 to 18 stitches per inch) when sewing on paper templates. As each template is pieced, reposition it on the master pattern. Because of the mirror imaging, it must be placed upside down.

7. String piece the *b* templates by using random top pressed-piecing (see Appendix, page 145), with the shiny side of the freezer paper up. Use the 1½" strips of graduated colors, following the color placement diagram and master pattern.

Your piecing will be more interesting if you sew strips on the diagonal, relative to the edge of the template. When angling the strips around a curve, allow the extra length of the strip to overhang the out-

side edge of the curve Fig. 2–15. This method will ensure that, when the strip is folded back and pressed, you will have plenty of fabric to cover the foundation. Again, reposition the piece on the master pattern.

8. Lay the *c* templates shiny side down on the wrong side of the appropriate fabrics and press with a dry iron to adhere the paper to the fabric. Cut the piece ¼" outside the template on all sides. For ease in stitching the curved seams, it will be necessary to remove the template from at least one side of the seam, so draw a sewing line on the fabric at each edge of the template, transferring the registration marks. Join the c pieces into units, following the piecing-order numbers on the master pattern.

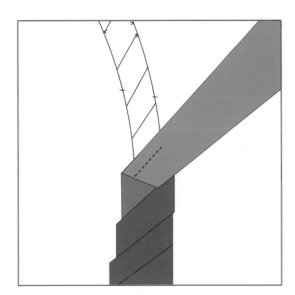

Fig. 2–15. Top press-piecing an outside curve.

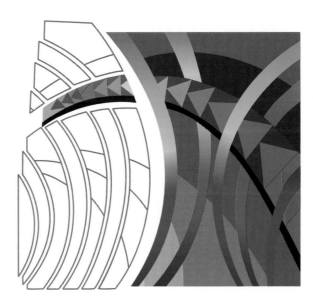

Fig. 2–16. Piecing progression.

9. Assemble the quilt in sections, adding pieced *a* and *b* segments to the *c* units (Fig. 2–16, page 37). Follow the piecing-order numbers, working from shorter to longer seams. There are no set-in seams, but every seam is slightly curved. To control the points in the *a* segments and maintain the smooth lines of the thin *b* segments, keep the foundations in place on the *a* and *b* units and stitch with the *a* or *b* side up, easing the *c* segments to fit the sewing lines.

10. When the top is complete, sew the four black border strips to the quilt, butting the corners. Layer the quilt top, batting, and backing, then baste the layers together. Quilt the layers with red, blue, and black thread (Fig. 2–17). Bind the raw edges with red binding.

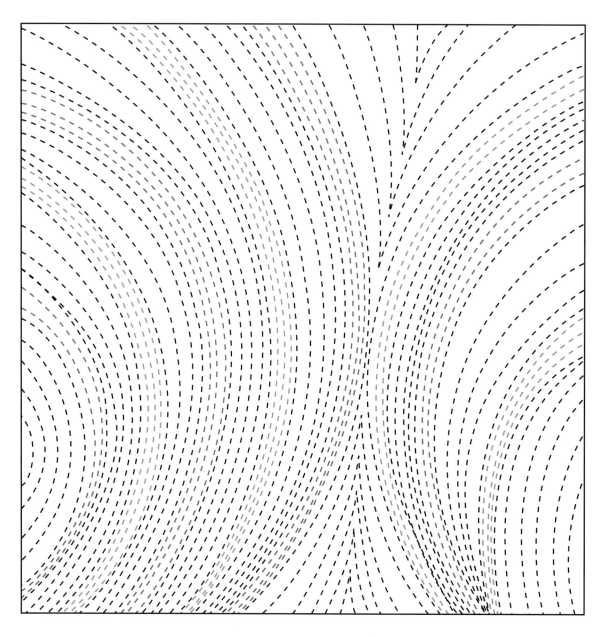

Fig. 2–17. Quilting design.

FLYING GEESE AND RAINBOWS pattern layout

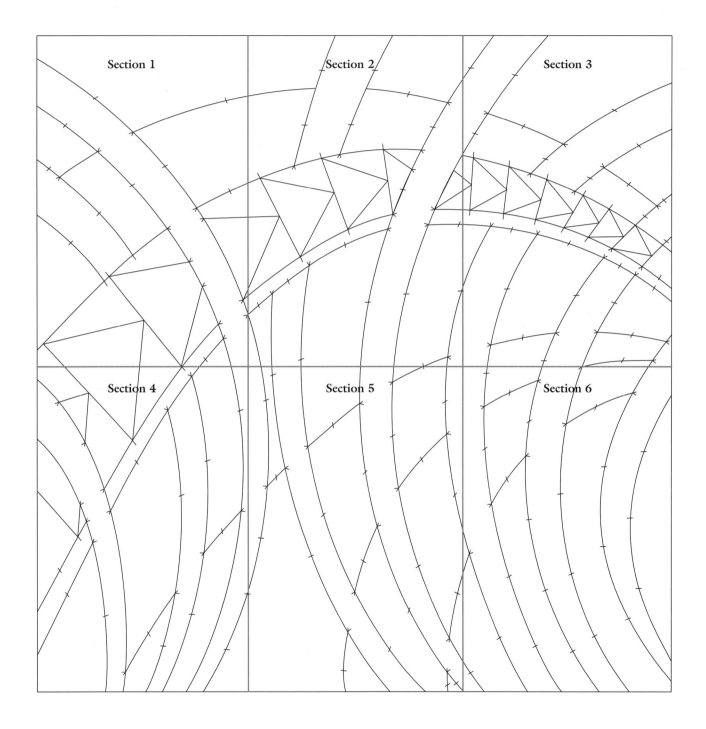

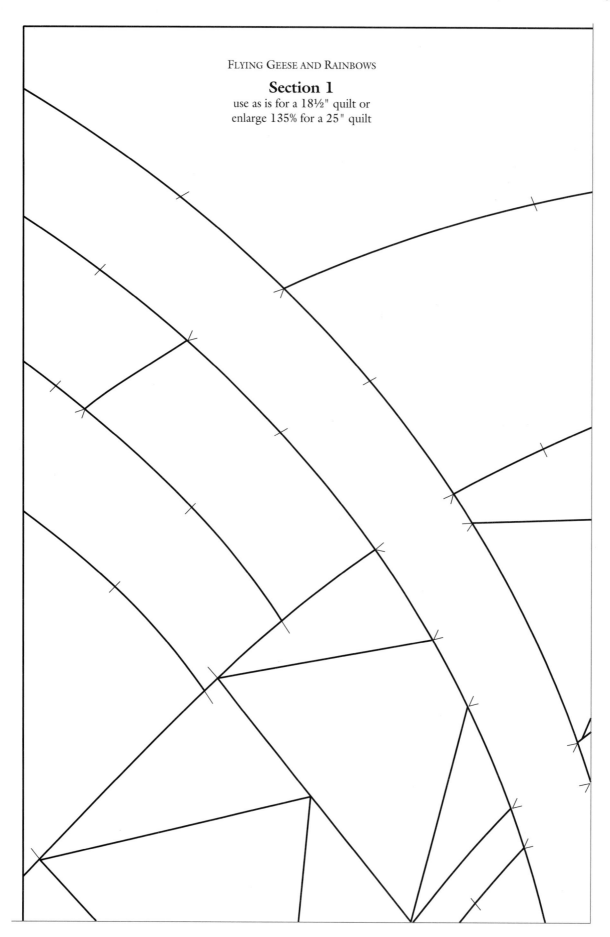

FLYING GEESE AND RAINBOWS

Section 1

use as is for a 18½" quilt or
enlarge 135% for a 25" quilt

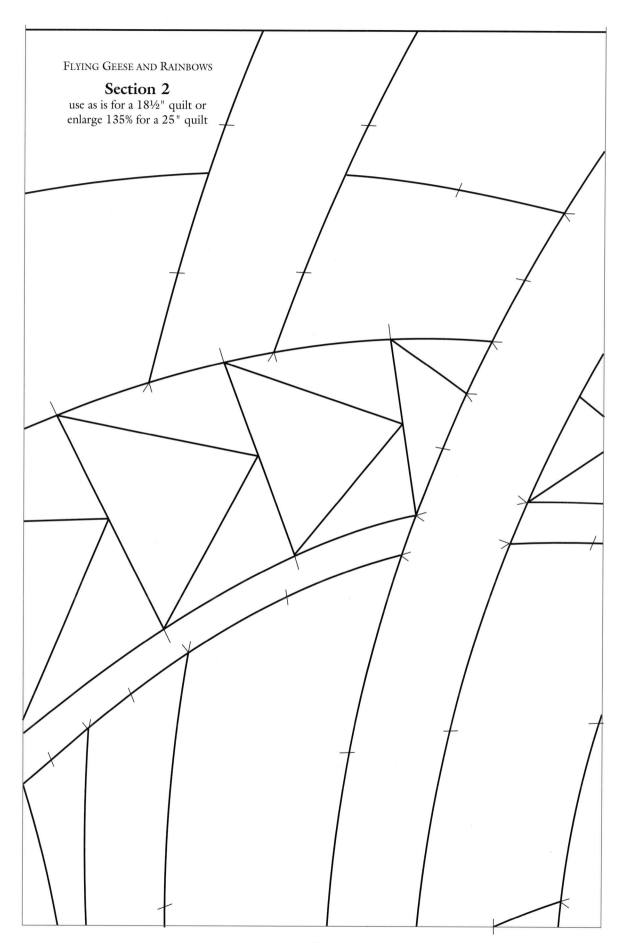

FLYING GEESE AND RAINBOWS

Section 2
use as is for a 18½" quilt or
enlarge 135% for a 25" quilt

FLYING GEESE AND RAINBOWS
Section 3
use as is for a 18½" quilt or
enlarge 135% for a 25" quilt

FLYING GEESE AND RAINBOWS

Section 4
use as is for a 18½" quilt or
enlarge 135% for a 25" quilt

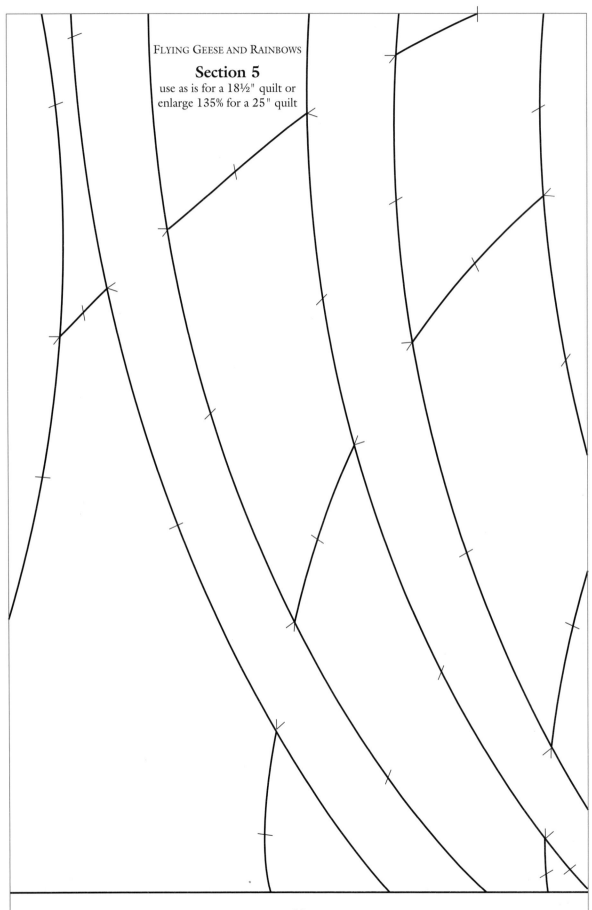

Flying Geese and Rainbows
Section 5
use as is for a 18½" quilt or
enlarge 135% for a 25" quilt

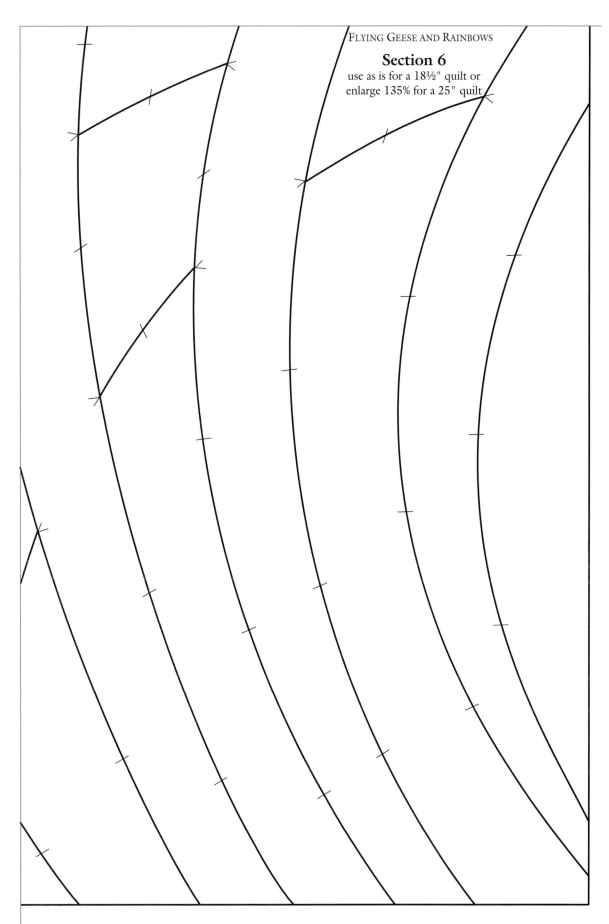

FLYING GEESE AND RAINBOWS

Section 6
use as is for a 18½" quilt or
enlarge 135% for a 25" quilt

Chapter 3
Crazy Quilts

There are many similarities between crazy and string quilts. Both were generally constructed of random fabric cuts on a foundation and made with a range of fabrics that include cotton, silk, and wool. Some string quilts, especially those made from silk, were embellished with embroidery. Some crazy quilts, often made of cotton, were not. Strings were not always cut perfectly straight, and crazy patching did not always consist of odd-shaped chunks of fabric. Many of each type of quilt combine both kinds of cuts.

The fine line between crazy quilts and string piecing is reinforced by a quilt made around 1890 (Photo 3–1). A combination string and crazy quilt, it is an example of multiple colors and values, with a prechosen selection of color. It looks as contemporary as if it were designed today.

Photo 3–1

full quilt on page 50

The public perception that crazy quilts are more elegant and less practical is generally true, especially those made at the height of the Victorian crazy-quilt fad. There was often a class difference between women who needed quickly made bedding for a growing family and those who had the leisure and money to lavishly embellish fine fabric with thread, ribbon, and paint merely to decorate their parlors.

Dixie recalls speaking to non-quilting community groups in Oklahoma who were unfamiliar with crazy quilts but who were very aware of string quilts because many had grown up with them. That makes sense, because Oklahoma was not opened to non-Native American settlement until 1889. This late date for immigration and settlement, right at the height of the Victorian crazy-quilt period, left the average pioneer with precious little time for the luxury of making non-functional quilts from fancy fabrics.

Speculation by early quilt historians that crazy quilts were one of the earliest type of quilts made in America has now been discounted. The theory that there were no crazy quilts in existance before the 1870s because they were all used up has been replaced with the more logical deduction that no earlier quilts have been found because none were made.

Crazy quilts, like string quilts, are now generally dated from the 1870s, although there are a few examples said to have been made earlier in the century. The peak of both popularity and

spectacular execution of the embellished crazy quilts was in the 1880–1910 period. Like their cousins, string quilts, their ascendency was aided by the wider availability of fabric, including silk, as well as the growth and advances in fabric manufacture and marketing. As the crazy-quilt fashion took hold, department stores and ads in ladies' magazines offered bags of silk, velvet, and ribbon scraps, often with instructions for crazy-quilt construction and embellishment.

Penny McMorris, in *Crazy Quilts*, attributes a major design source for these pieces to the widespread interest in Japanese arts and culture at that time. The Japanese Pavilion at the 1876 Centennial Exposition in Philadelphia caused a sensation, revealing what was a new part of the world to most Americans. The asymmetric designs, irregular shapes, and crazed compositions were embellished with fans and floral motifs, worked with thread, ribbons, and paint. Plain cotton calicoes quickly took a back seat to the lure of working with elegant fabrics and adornments.

In addition to the types and cuts of fabrics, the biggest difference between these two styles was their method of construction. The pressed-piecing technique used for string quilts could only be done with fabric pieces with relatively straight edges. An early quilt top that bridges the

gap between string and crazy piecing was press-pieced by hand on muslin foundations (Photo 3–2). The combination of strings and irregularly shaped pieces of fabric give it a crazy-quilt look, but it is all straight-line pressed-piecing with no curves, and it was obviously not intended to be embellished. Many of the cotton fabrics are from the late third quarter of the nineteenth century, just before the fancy fabric, embellished style of crazy piecing took hold, but the design of some of the blocks was obviously influenced by that form.

Photo 3–2
detail
*full quilt on
page 50*

Conversely, most of the crazy quilts made during the peak of their popularity were not press-pieced, but rather made as appliqué collages, which allowed the use of curved and odd-shaped chunks of fabric. The design was completely composed, and the fabrics were basted on the foundation with the raw edges turned under before they were stitched permanently to the foundation, with embroidery. Two pieced blocks from the Victorian period illustrate the elaborate embroidery and elegant fabrics of the classic crazy quilt (Photo 3–3). Basting stitches holding the fabrics in place for embellishment are still visible.

Photo 3–3

full block on page 50

Our first project (page 57) is a miniature replica of a quilt in the Historic Pensacola Village collection, circa 1880, a composition of small squares running diagonally across the blocks. Guest artist Nancy Davison faithfully reproduced the fabric, colors, and embellishments of the original.

As the crazy-quilt era declined, simpler shapes replaced the curves and asymmetrical forms favored earlier, and fancy fabrics were replaced by more ordinary ones, such as wool and cotton. Jane's late nineteenth-century cotton crazy-quilt top is a compendium of cotton fabrics of the era (Photo 3–4). The elongated chunks and large strips of bright fabrics are appliquéd to the foundations with a straight stitch on a sewing machine and contain no embellishment. The foundations are waste fabric, in many cases made of several pieces. It's interesting to speculate that, as access to sewing machines increased, women looked for construction techniques like pressed-piecing or top-stitching, which were more easily done by machine.

Photo 3–4

full quilt on page 51

Crazy piecing, like string piecing, can be done as easily on variously shaped foundations as on square ones. An eight-pointed-star quilt top contains diamond-shaped foundations of muslin, covered with both string and crazy piecing (Photo 3–5). Hand stitching is used for both the pressed-piecing and the traditional appliqué collage applied to each foundation.

Photo 3–5

full quilt on page 51

Triangular shapes are combined with squares in Betty Verhoeven's A BIG FAN OF CRAZY QUILTS, a silk medallion crazy quilt that exhibits Victorian styling in a contemporary application (Photo 3–6). Embroidery and embellishment, including a dramatic spider web in the center of the quilt, show the continued appeal of this type of crazy quilting.

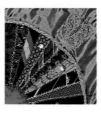

Photo 3–6

full quilt on page 51

Alice Kolb's project, THIS, THAT, AND THE OTHER (page 61), updates the Victorian crazy-quilt style for today's quiltmakers working entirely with the sewing machine. She uses the traditional technique of appliqué collage, laying down the pieces initially with machine straight stitching. The process is completed with wonderful machine embroidery and embellishments.

In contrast, Lynn Graves's project, CRAZY STAINED GLASS (page 65) was made entirely with pressed-piecing and no appliqué. She inserts flat piping between each pressed-pieced seam for her machine crazy piecing. The piping frames and accents the shapes, giving a stained-glass look to the random shapes and colors.

While many quilters continue to think of crazy quilts as a way to use elegant fabric and embellishment, others are using a non-embellished design technique to combine fabric in a non-structured arrangement, in effect creating their own fabric. Dixie uses pressed-piecing as the main construction technique, reserving appliqué for special effects. She likes to use non-embellished crazy piecing to add texture and dimension, combined with different fabric formulas to achieve different effects. The formulas include the following formats:

Same fabric. Covering a foundation with crazy piecing made with one solid fabric maintains the impact of a single color, while the seams of the piecing create a texture that could not be achieved by quilting alone. Cutting the fabric at various angles, a natural result of crazy piecing, results in subtle shading. The shading is more pronounced with fabrics that are polished, brushed, or blended.

Various prints, same color and value. Using these prints creates interesting fabric texture with a single color focus. For the best effect, use fabrics with a variety of scales and patterns.

Same color, different values. This approach can be done with prints, solids, or a combination of both. It adds texture and motion, while retaining the general effect of a single color.

Two-color prints. A collection of fabrics with the same two colors in each fabric can create an interesting and vibrant accent especially when used with other areas made in the same color and value or the same color with different values.

Multiple colors and values. This is the traditional combination for crazy piecing. It can range from using every fabric in the scrap bag to controlling the palette with a prechosen combination of compatible fabrics. It can be pieced from all prints, all solids, or a combination of both.

When embellishments are used, solids may be necessary to avoid losing the embellishments in the riot of color and fabric.

REDCUBES was constructed with same-fabric crazy piecing to create a contemporary composition with a dimensional effect (Photo 3–7). The geometric cubist design has both balance and focus. The effect of light hitting the differently positioned grain lines of the fabrics is striking.

Photo 3–7

full quilt on page 52

The background for the various appliquéd shorthand expressions of DESIGN FOR LIFE was crazy pieced in the same color and value (Photo 3–8). Both the combination used in this quilt and same-fabric piecing make interesting backgrounds for either piecing or appliqué, providing a rich texture not attainable with a plain piece of fabric.

Photo 3–8

full quilt on page 52

CRAZY CRACKER, our final project in this chapter (page 69), is made with crazy piecing on curved foundations based on

two of the fabric formulas. The gray and the black sections contain the same color and value of various prints. The black and white curves in the blocks and borders are made of a two-color print combination of fabrics.

Delores Hamilton's CRAZY QUILT FOR A CRAZY KID contains the classic combination of multiple prints and values for a dynamic, contemporary scrap-bag look. A planned border with same color and value piecing, made in paler colors, will calm this exuberance (Photo 3–9). She also used occasional pre-pieced segments to create units for pressed-piecing, providing extra texture and value changes.

Photo 3–9

larger photo on page 52

CELEBRATION 2000! was made by using three fabric formulas (Photo 3–10, page 53). Most of the fan-shaped foundations that form circular shapes behind the four-pointed stars are constructed of the same color and value, while one has a two-color combination. A few have the same-color/different-value formula, as does the border, to provide extra texture and movement. The border was chosen to reinforce the crazy piecing within the quilt while highlighting the yellow stars.

Photo 3–1. (LEFT) Antique string-crazy quilt, 38" x 72", circa 1890. Maker unknown. From the collection of Julia S. Wernicke.

Photo 3–2. (RIGHT) Antique string-crazy quilt cotton top, 76" x 84", circa 1885. Maker unknown. From the collection of Kathlyn Sullivan.

Photo 3–3. Two antique crazy-quilt blocks, circa 1890. Maker unknown. From the collection of Dixie Haywood.

Photo 3–4. Antique cotton non-embellished crazy quilt, machine top-stitched, 84" x 90", circa 1910. Maker unknown. From the collection of Jane Hall.

Photo 3–5. Antique eight-pointed-star, crazy-quilt top, 81" x 82", circa 1900. Maker unknown. From the collection of Jane Hall.

Photo 3–6. BIG FAN OF CRAZY QUILTS, 74" x 74", 1996. Made by Betty Verhoeven.

Photo 3–8. DESIGN FOR LIFE, 24" x 32", 1999. Made by Dixie Haywood.

Photo 3–7. REDCUBES, 69" x 84", 1985. Made by Dixie Haywood.

Photo 3–9. (LEFT) CRAZY QUILT FOR A CRAZY KID, detail, 105" x 105", 1999. Made by Delores Hamilton.

Photo 3–10. CELEBRATION 2000!, 87" x 87", 1999. Made by Dixie Haywood.

Photo 3–10

full quilt on page 53

Crazy piecing, regardless of style and coloration, adapts well to clothing, offering a designer look suitable for a variety of personal styles. Darts and tucks can be taken without disrupting a more structured block pattern, and crazy piecing does not look truncated when cut into the variously shaped pattern pieces. When making a crazy-pieced garment (especially on a permanent foundation) that is close fitting, cut the foundation a little larger than the pattern and use the pattern piece to cut it to size after piecing.

Crazy Quilt Projects

Explore the following projects to whet your appetite for this ever-changing design category. Whether embellished Victorian crazy quilts are your passion, or you want to investigate contemporary uses of the technique by hand or by machine, you will find a quilt to engage your hands and mind. All the projects were sewn by machine, on varying types of foundations, and embellished and quilted both by hand and machine.

General Crazy Piecing Directions

This is a true design-in-the-cloth technique, a free-form random romp with fabric. To become familiar with these directions, we suggest you make a practice block (Photo 3–11) and then make another one. It becomes easier and more fun each time you do it. The suggested technique is random top pressed-piecing.

Photo 3–11 Sample crazy-quilt block.

1. Cut a foundation to the desired shape. Select the fabrics to be used, and cut the first piece in a size proportionate to the foundation. Pin the piece on top of the foundation, with the right side up (Fig. 3–1a).

2. Lay a second piece of fabric along one edge of the first piece, right side down, and sew through all layers with a small stitch and an approximate ¼" seam allowance. Do not sew beyond either end of the underneath piece (Fig. 3–1b).

3. Press open the fabric firmly and cut to the desired shape. Cut even with or within the boundaries formed by the other edges of the first piece, indicated by the dashed lines in the figure, to avoid an inside angle that cannot be stitched in a straight line. Pin the piece just added to the

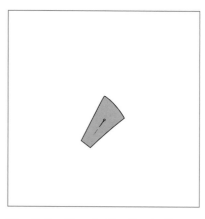

Fig. 3–1a. Piece 1. Shading in figures 3-1a–h indicates piece being added.

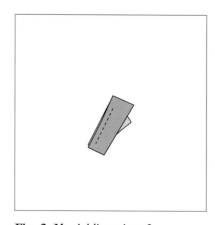

Fig. 3–1b. Adding piece 2.

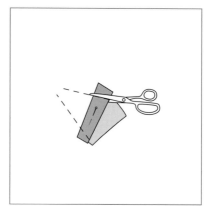

Fig. 3–1c. Cut piece 2 to the desired shape, making sure it does not extend past the edges of piece 1.

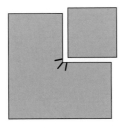

Fig. 3–1d. To create a curve, cut a right angle from the fabric. Clip the angle to make the curve lie flat.

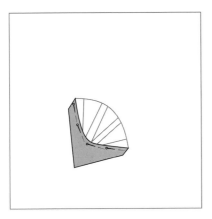

Fig. 3–1e. Turn under the allowance along the curve and pin. Cut piece to the desired shape.

foundation to avoid its slipping or puckering when the next piece is added (Fig. 3–1c). Continue adding pieces by sewing, opening, pressing, and cutting. Move around the shape to avoid piecing repeatedly on the same side.

4. To cut a curve, start by cutting out a right angle from the fabric (Fig. 3–1d). Clip at the angle to make the curve lie flat. Turn under a seam allowance as you fit the curve over the previously sewn fabric.

5. Pin the curve in place before cutting the remainder of the shape (Fig. 3–1e). These shapes are most effective when the angle of the cut echoes the highest point of the curve. Small curves are easiest to sew by hand, either with embroidery or invisible hand or machine appliqué.

6. With care, long sweeping curves can be stitched by machine. To do so, position the curve with the seam allowance pressed under. Carefully

slip pins into the folds at right angles to the curve. Anchor the pins in the turned-under allowance only, being careful not to catch the fabric on top (Fig. 3–1f).

7. Sew the curve, taking care not to shift the pinned edge. Stitch along the pressed fold (Fig. 3–1g). Remove the pins. Trim excess fabric from underneath the curve. Press open and cut the piece to the desired shape (Fig. 3–1h).

8. Curves can also be cut from fabric that has already been sewn in place. Follow the same procedure, described in step six. Then place fabric underneath the curve and pin in place. This type of curve works best when started from a long line, and it needs to be closed with embroidery or invisible appliqué.

9. Triple curves create an effective design focus. Start with a single sweeping curve, as described in steps five and six. Cut two more curves, one

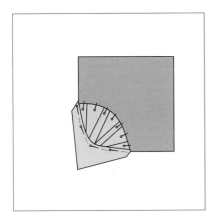

Fig. 3–1f. Turn allowance under and anchor pins in allowance only.

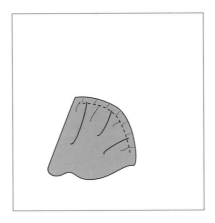

Fig. 3–1g. With pieces right sides together, sew curve.

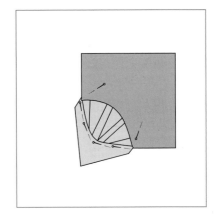

Fig. 3–1h. Finished curve. Use pins to hold in place.

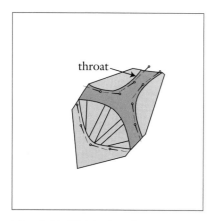

Fig. 3–1i. Finished triple curve.

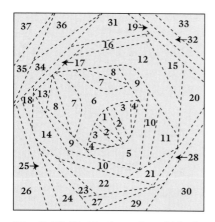

Fig. 3–1j. Finished numbered block.

on each side of the first curve. Take into consideration that a seam allowance will be needed on either side of the "throat" and do not cut it too narrow (Fig. 3–1i). If in doubt, draw the angles with chalk to visualize the width of the throat before you cut. These curves also must be closed with embroidery or invisible appliqué.

10. Continue adding pieces, making sure the fabric extends beyond the edges of the foundation. Trim the fabric to a ¼" seam allowance on all edges.

Tips and Tricks

1. With experience, it is easy – and fun – to experiment with fabric and color placement, slants and angles, and the positioning of different cuts of the same fabric. Beginning crazy-quilt piecers are sometimes uneasy with the process of designing in the cloth and positioning, stitching, and cutting as they go. The unplanned and unmarked method can cause insecurity and undermine their confidence in the success of the process. Initially, it may be helpful to draw some basic placement lines on the foundation before stitching, because we are familiar with

drawn lines and seem to be able to visualize the outcome better. However, don't become dependent on pre-planned crazy piecing. Learn to enjoy the spontaneity of designing as you go.

2. Consider the fabric when making cuts. Cutting a long narrow strip along a stripe can reinforce the fabric pattern with the cut. Cutting across a stripe on an angle can add an edgy, vibrant accent.

3. Because the foundation provides stability, you can generally disregard grain lines when making cuts. However, long narrow cuts are easier to sew when they are on grain. If they have been cut along the bias, pin with special care to avoid twisting.

4. As you continue to piece, some of the lines formed will grow quite long. To remedy this, sew a piece of fabric along all the strips and then make two or more angled cuts, creating a triangle. See piece #22 or 34 in Fig. 3–1j.

5. The effect of a curve can be achieved without actually making one. Simply stitch two pieces of the same fabric so they cross on either side of a patch, and the eye will see a curve.

Miniature Crazy Quilt

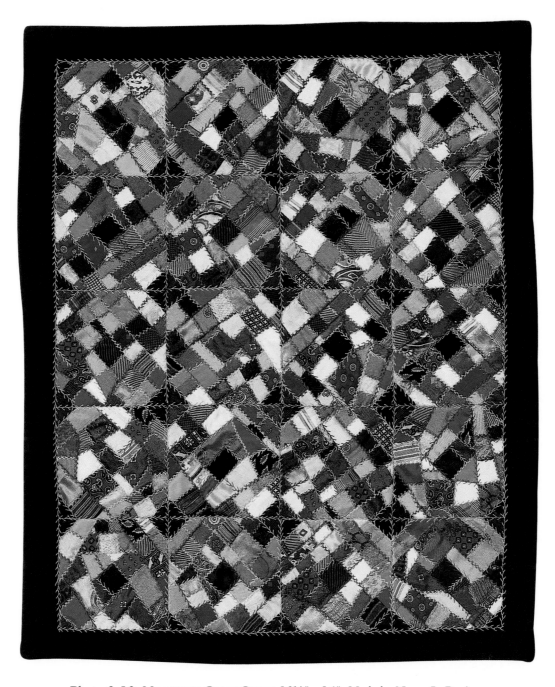

Photo 3–12. MINIATURE CRAZY QUILT, 13½" x 16". Made by Nancy L. Davison.

Learn to work small, even with slippery, difficult-to-control fabrics. Nancy developed some great tips to make it easier to piece this miniature replica of a crazy quilt in the Historic Pensacola Village collection. Like the original, this quilt has dark corner triangles echoing the dark center squares in the blocks, with random pre-pieced patches surrounding the centers for an interesting fractured look with somewhat controlled values.

TECHNIQUE:
Random Top Pressed-Piecing,
   some Under Pressed-Piecing

SIZE:
13½" x 16"

BLOCKS:
Twenty 3" (finished) blocks

BORDER:
¾" (finished)

MATERIALS:
Bits and pieces of a wide variety of lightweight silky fabrics ("a lapful")

1 yard lightweight unbleached muslin for foundations, washed and ironed

⅝ yard dark, lightweight silk or silk-like fabric for borders and backing

Superfine sharp pins

Permanent fabric marker

Six-strand embroidery floss in a variety of colors

#9 Crewel/embroidery needle

Usual sewing supplies

FABRIC NOTE: Use a large variety of silky solid colors, tiny Paisley prints, small geometric prints, and narrow stripes. Wider stripes can be used to simulate two patches by embroidering over the line between them. Nancy doesn't recommend velvets for work in this scale, but a velvet effect could be achieved with lightweight synthetic suede-cloth. Use as many different fabrics as possible. Forty or fifty would not be too many.

Nancy primarily used silk neckties, along with selected blends of similar weights. She divided the ties into darks, mediums, and lights, and machine washed each value group on a gentle cycle with a fine-fabric detergent and a short spin in the dryer on the delicate setting. She discarded any ties distressed by the laundering process as well as the middle section of the tie that knots around the neck. The wide end was cut open along the seam on the back, and the lining and interlining were thrown away. Stains or snags, which were easy to spot as she pressed the fabrics, were cut out. Nancy stored the narrow ends for another project and added additional colors and textures from a collection of silk-like fabric to fill any gaps the neckties didn't supply.

Construction

1. Tape the muslin to your worktable. Using a permanent pen, draw 3" squares separated by 1" spaces. Mark the horizontal and vertical center lines through all the squares and mark the triangles at the corners to position the patches (Fig. 3–2). Cut out the squares, with ½" seam allowances to make the small foundations easy to handle during the piecing process. The quilt requires 20 squares. Nancy prepared three or four extras so she could discard any "mistakes" rather than try to fix them.

2. Cut the silky fabrics into pieces about 1" square, better a bit too large than too small. Don't try for perfect squares. The silk is slinky and will creep and crawl as you cut. The more lopsided pieces will help create a crazy-quilt look.

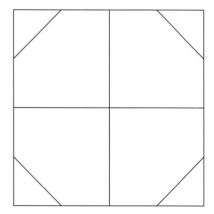

Fig. 3–2. MINIATURE CRAZY QUILT block marking diagram.

3. Pin the patches together in pairs and chain-stitch 20 or 30 pairs at a time. Use some dark solid fabrics, such as black, navy, maroon, or dark green, for one side of some of the pairs to act as a center block. Trim the seam allowances to a scant ¼", press the pairs open, and scatter them on a tray.

4. Pin the dark half of a pair at the center of a foundation on the unmarked side, with the square on point. The markings on the foundations are used as guides for placing the centers and for joining the blocks. Only the corner triangle markings are used as specific sewing lines for under pressed-piecing.

5. Working around the center, add fabric pairs, trimming as necessary to achieve a somewhat skewed line. Nancy likes the strips to be "wayward" for an unplanned effect. She works on several blocks at one time to keep from over-planning. Press after each addition. At some point, triple and quadruple assemblies of patches will need to be pre-pieced to fit the lines. Occasionally, you will need to make a five-patch strip. Be selective about colors and values but try for as much variety as possible, with a balance of solids, prints, and stripes.

6. As you approach the corners, trim the patches to prepare for positioning the dark triangle, making sure that the fabrics cover the sewing line with an adequate seam allowance. Cut the triangles oversized to avoid fitting problems. Pin the triangle in place, turn the block over, and sew on the marked corner lines with under pressed-piecing.

7. As you piece, your skills and interpretation of the design will change, and the scale of the blocks and the color placement may vary. Wait until they are all pieced to arrange them, balancing the total effect of colors and values (Fig. 3–3).

8. Stabilize the edges of the blocks by stay-stitching in the seam allowances. Trim the seam allowances to ¼". Stitch the blocks together along the marked lines on the backs of the foundations.

9. Cut four border strips 1¼" wide and attach them to the quilt, butting the corners. Embroider the quilt (see About Embroidery, page 60).

10. Lay the backing, right side down, on top of the quilt and sew around the edge, leaving an opening. Turn the quilt right side out and close the opening by hand. Attach the layers together with ties on the back that catch only the foundation layer. To prevent the backing from rolling at the edge, quilt at the inside edge of the border from the back with small stitches, also catching only the foundation layer.

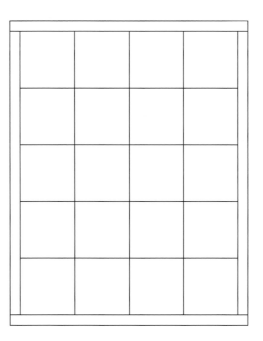

Fig. 3–3. MINIATURE CRAZY QUILT layout.

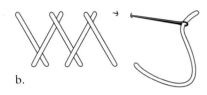

Figure 3–4. Embroidery stitches: a. feather stitch, b. herringbone stitch.

About Embroidery

Two stitches that work well in a small scale are shown in Figures 3–4 a and b. Use a single strand of embroidery floss and a crewel needle. Choose a thread color that will be effective on the fabrics it will cover. Don't pull your stitches too tight to avoid puckering. In the quilt in the photo, the seams joining the blocks and border were embroidered with the feather stitch in gold floss. The seams within the blocks were embroidered in a wide variety of colors with both stitches.

Nancy advises that you not do all the embroidery in one area. Scatter the embellishments while your skills increase and your understanding of the colors and the project grows. This approach will give the finished quilt a more balanced look. Remember that rules are meant to be broken and follow your instincts if you have mastered another stitch, if you have a bright idea, or if you just feel adventurous.

MINIATURE CRAZY QUILT block.

This, That, and the Other

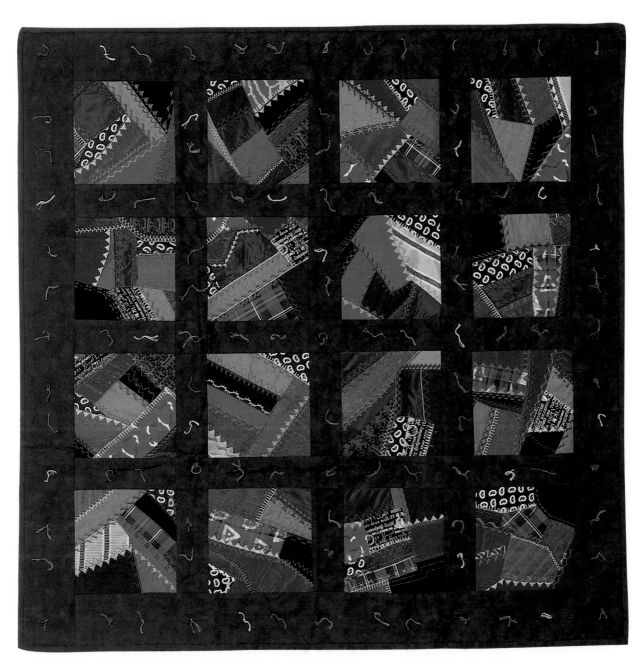

Photo 3–13. THIS, THAT, AND THE OTHER, 36" x 36". Made by Alice Allen Kolb.

Modern approaches to traditional crazy-quilt techniques are easily achievable with the sewing machine and its vast array of stitches. In fact, the innovations in stitches, functions, types of threads and stabilizers, all designed to make the sewing process easier, also help us to focus on the creativity more than the process. Quilts or throws, clothing accents, and accessories for wearables or home decorating are good choices for this kind of crazy quilting.

Photo 3–13

detail

full quilt on page 61

Alice's contemporary technique involves stitching fabrics to a muslin foundation with straight-stitch appliqué. The straight stitches are easily concealed by machine decorative stitches, used just like traditional hand embroidery stitches. She often sews in multiple rows of colors, overlaying and grouping a wide variety of stitches in different weights and textures of threads. The decorative imagery is accented with hand beading, vintage buttons, and random ribbons.

TECHNIQUE:
Straight-Stitch Machine
   Appliqué

QUILT SIZE:
36" x 36"

BLOCKS:
Sixteen 6" (finished) blocks

BORDERS:
2" (finished) sashing and corner
   squares between blocks
3" (finished) borders

MATERIALS:
Assorted cottons, silks, and
   hand-dyed fabrics to equal 2
   yards

Complementary solid cotton
   fabric for sashing and borders
   – 1¼ yard

Muslin for foundations – 1¼
   yard

Backing – 1¼ yard

Binding – ⅜ yard

Optional low-loft batting

THREADS:
All-purpose neutral blending
   thread in two colors, beige or
   gray for stitching light fabrics
   and a dark, neutral color for
   dark fabrics

Decorative threads in assorted
   complementary colors (ray-
   ons, cottons, topstitch, metallic, plus braids and decorative
   ribbons)

MACHINE EMBROIDERY
SUPPLIES:
Sewing machine with decora-
   tive stitches

Embroidery foot (open-toed is
   best)

Embroidery darning foot for
   free-motion stitching

Braiding or couching foot

Sewing machine embroidery
   #75/90 needles for lightweight threads

Topstitch #100 needles for top-
   stitch and metallic threads

Lightweight tear-away stabilizer
   to support decorative stitches

Second bobbin case – reserve
   for threads too thick and rav-
   elly to sew through the eye
   of a sewing machine needle.
   (Adjust set-screw tension on
   this bobbin case only. Leave
   other bobbin case set for normal thread.)

Special trims, buttons, ribbons

Embroidery floss for tying the
   finished quilt

Spray starch

Usual sewing supplies

Construction

1. Cut 16 muslin foundations 6½" x 6½". There is no need to mark stitching lines. This is a design-as-you-go technique.

2. Select a variety of fabrics for the first block. Spray-starch the pieces to give the fabric body for machine stitching.

3. For fabric #1, cut an uneven patch with straight sides to fit over one corner of the first foundation. Select fabric #2, creating a seam line by folding one side under ¼" and pin the piece over one side of the first patch through all the layers. Repeat this process, adding new patches over the raw edges of the patch shapes until the muslin square is covered (Fig. 3–5). Trim away excess fabric bulk under the pieces as necessary. If you want a patch to appear smaller, apply the next piece of fabric over part of it and trim the surplus from the underneath the patch. Working this way will allow you to compose the entire piece, controlling the lines, angles, and curves before stitching.

4. Add ribbons and trims under the edges of the patch seams as desired.

5. Secure the patches to the muslin with straight-stitch appliqué. Use a continuous line of straight stitching, beginning at an outside edge. Stitch from one fabric patch to another as far as possible, pivoting as needed to sew the next patch. When you hit a dead end, stop and backstitch two stitches, raise the presser foot, and move to the next obvious place to stitch. There may be areas that will have to be stitched independently.

Decorative Stitching

1. Sew with the lighter weight threads in assorted stitches over the straight-stitch lines. Alice recommends starting with the quieter, simpler stitches. Select stitches that are kindred in spirit to the fabric, such as blanket stitches, feather and cross stitches, and zigzags.

2. Successful stitching is best achieved by first making a "personal insurance plan." Sew a stitch sample on a scrap of muslin to check the appearance, color choice, and tension. Fine-tune the color and stitch selection from this sample. Use strips of a tear-away stabilizer under the actual stitching line to prevent the stitches from rippling or bunching.

3. To give a nostalgic look to the unit, consider using a different stitch design on either side of the fabric edges, with a dense narrow satin stitch down the seam center. With two or three patterns in different colors and images, the threads are not only attractive, but in keeping with tradition.

4. For top stitching and metallic threads, use a large-eyed, top-stitch needle and set the stitch length longer. Heavier

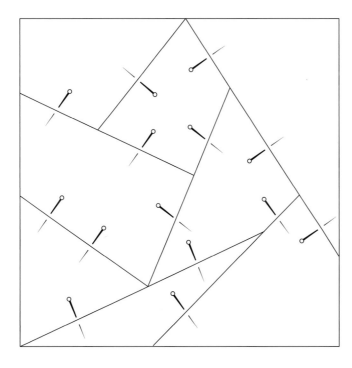

Fig. 3–5. Fabrics pinned and ready to stitch.

threads can be sewn randomly across two or more patches.

5. It is easy to sew with the decorative threads in the bobbin, but remember that the bobbin does not hold much thread, so design your stitching accordingly. It is fun, experimental, and true "play." With decorative threads in the bobbin, sew with the crazy patch right side down against the throat plate. Stitch a simple decorative stitch along the straight-stitch appliqué line. The beautiful thread will then show on the patched side. If the stitch isn't as attractive as you would like, loosen the bobbin screw a quarter turn. (A cue for bobbin screw adjustment is "lefty-loosey, righty-tighty.")

6. Couched threads are easily sewn with a braiding foot. Insert braid into the hole in the toe and sew across the patch in random fashion. Motif patterns are best applied to the patches before "pin-piecing" them to the foundation. Stitch a stack of assorted motifs and letters, and select and insert them as you crazy-patch. Buttons and trinkets are generally added after the quilt has been pieced and squared, but before the binding is added.

7. Square the finished blocks to 6½" each. Remove the stabilizers as much as possible.

8. Cut 24 strips of sashing fabric, 2½" x 6½". Cut nine corner squares 2½" x 2½". Cut four borders 3½" x 36½". Assemble the quilt in rows, adding the borders and butting the corners (Fig. 3–6). Measure and square up the quilt.

9. Using batting (optional), layer and baste the quilt. Tie the layers with embroidery floss in a random arrangement, placing ties at each sashing intersection or in each crazy patch as desired. Bind the quilt's raw edges. Be sure to sign and date your quilt, either on a crazy patch or a label for the back of the quilt.

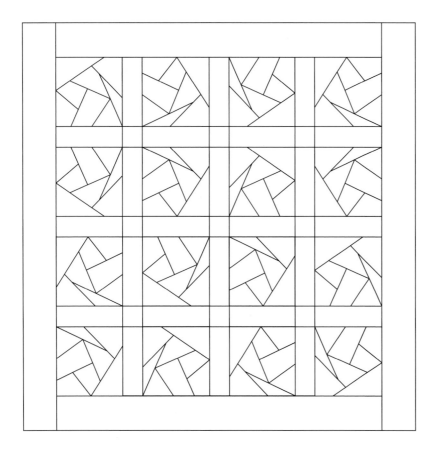

Fig. 3–6. THIS, THAT, AND THE OTHER layout.

Crazy Stained Glass

Photo 3–14. CRAZY STAINED GLASS, 33" x 42". Designed by Lynn Graves, pieced and quilted by Marion Wolpert.

The beautiful stained-glass look of this contemporary crazy quilt comes from the addition of flat piping in the seams as embellishment. It can be made with scraps or planned yardage. The quilt, designed by Lynn Graves, was pieced and quilted by Marion Wolpert, and was made with a pack of 12 fat-quarters of hand-dyed fabric.

TECHNIQUE:
Precise Top Pressed-Piecing

SIZE:
33" x 42"

BLOCKS:
Twelve 7" (finished) blocks

BORDERS:
2" (finished) sashing and inner borders
2" (finished) pieced outer border with crazy-quilt fabrics

MATERIALS:
¼-yard pieces of 12 different solid-colored fabrics, total of 3 yards

Two yards black fabric for piping, sashes, inner border, and binding

1½ yards backing fabric

Batting

Silk thread for machine quilting

Spray starch

Usual sewing supplies

Cutting Directions

Black fabric

Fifteen 1" strips, cut from the length of the fabric, for piping. *Note:* you may need more, depending on the number and sizes of the pieces you use in each block.
Eight 2½" x 7½" black vertical sashes
Three 2½" x 25½" black horizontal sashes
Two 2½" x 34½" black vertical borders
Two 2½" x 29½" black horizontal borders

Crazy quilt fabrics

One 2½" strip and one 4" strip from each fabric. If you are using scraps, they must have at least one straight edge.

Construction

1. Prepare 12 foundations the size of the finished block (page 68). The block pattern is intended to be just a guide. For this quilt, copy it 12 times or, to make the blocks slightly different from each other, change the shape or size of the center and any of the subsequent numbered pieces. Changes could be made by enlarging the pieces, by pre-piecing, or by combining or dividing pieces. Study Photo 3–14, page 65, to determine other designs for blocks with different lines, making sure not to stitch yourself into a corner. See the general Crazy Quilting directions, page 54.

2. Prepare flat piping by folding 1" strips in half lengthwise, wrong sides together, and pressing to make ½" piping strips. Stripes, wavy stripes, and directional fabric are other options for the piping, giving a whole new look to this design. *Tip:* Spray starch helps to stabilize the fabric.

3. Following the general crazy quilt directions, position the first piece of fabric on the foundation, right side up. The edges should be just inside the fabric placement line. The numbers on the pattern indicate the piecing order. The arrows show the sewing direction. Place a piece of flat piping on top of this fabric, with its edges at the line. Lynn uses a few dabs of fabric glue along the raw edges

to secure them. Place the second piece of fabric on top of the flat piping, again aligning all of the raw edges just inside the fabric placement line.

4. Stitch exactly ¼" from the fabric placement line, using a ¼" foot for accuracy. Lynn recommends a size 90/14 needle and 16 to 20 stitches per inch.

5. Open the second piece, press, and trim the edges so they are just inside the next fabric placement lines. Repeat layering the piping and fabrics at each seam line until the block is covered with fabric, with fabrics extending at least ¼" on all sides of the foundation.

6. To add another dimension to the piecing, pre-piece piping between the short ends of two strips, and sandwich the long edge of this pre-pieced fabric on the foundation with piping as usual. This allows a short line of piping to run perpendicularly or at an angle to the previous line of piping.

7. Using a ruler and rotary cutter, trim the blocks to measure 7½" x 7½". It is easiest and most accurate to do all 12 at the same time.

8. Arrange the blocks in a 3 x 4 grid, adding sashing (Fig. 3–7). Stitch the short vertical pieces first, then the long horizontal pieces. Add the two vertical inner borders, then the horizontal borders, butting the corners. True the measurements and the edges.

9. To make the pieced outer border, cut 2½" strips from the scraps of crazy quilt fabric. Cut these 3"–5" and stitch them together to make the vertical borders first, then the two horizontal borders.

10. Measure and square up the quilt. Layer, baste, and quilt by machine in the ditch around the edges of each block and along the edge of the flat piping in several places within each block. You need only enough quilting to anchor the layers because you don't want to distract from the stained-glass effect. Bind the raw edges with a double-fold, straight-grain binding, cut 2½" wide.

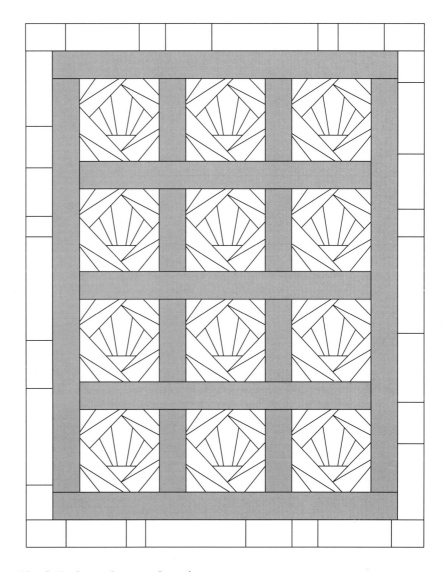

Fig. 3–7. Crazy Stained Glass layout.

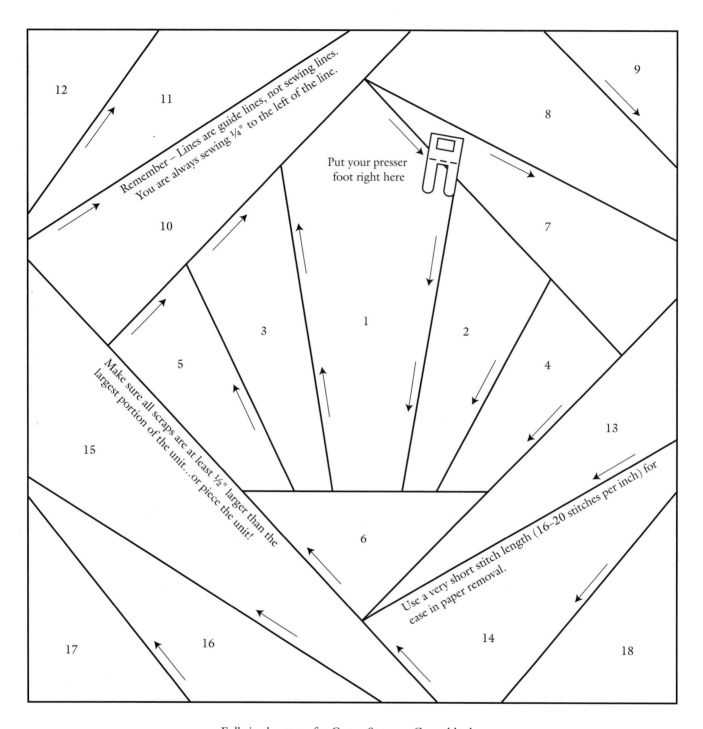

Full-sized pattern for CRAZY STAINED GLASS block.

Crazy Cracker

Photo 3–15. CRAZY CRACKER, 30" x 30". Made by Dixie Haywood.

This achromatic non-embellished crazy quilt is pieced from many prints of the same values in black, gray, and black-and-white sections. The curved border is an integral part of the quilt design. Silver metallic thread was used for the machine quilting so it would be more visible on the print fabric. Piping was used to finish the edges instead of bias binding. This quilt appears more complex than it is. Give it a try!

TECHNIQUE:
Random Top Pressed-Piecing

SIZE:
30" x 30"

BLOCKS:
Nine 7" (finished) blocks

MATERIALS:
Several prints in relatively the same values, but with different scale and density in each – a total of ¾ yard of black, gray, and black and white

Black solid fabric for piped edge – ½ yard to be cut on the bias

Backing fabric – 1 yard

Lightweight paper or interfacing for temporary foundations

Batting

Cable cord for edge – 4 yards, #5/32 size

Silver metallic thread for machine quilting, appropriate sewing machine needle

Usual sewing supplies

Construction

1. Cut foundations: nine 7" squares, and one 21" square cut twice diagonally to form four triangles for the corners.

2. Trace the block pattern (page 71) on four of the square foundations, numbering the pieces and drawing the registration lines on the back of the foundations. Mark pieces #1 and #3 "black" and piece #2 "black and white." Cut apart. Mark five remaining squares "gray."

3. Enlarge the corner triangle pattern on page 72 and transfer the curve to the foundations. To make the curve even, fold the corner piece in half, drawing half the curve and then tracing the second half. Mark the small triangle on the corner foundation, starting 7" from each end of the longest side of the pattern. Draw lines to a point 3½" up from the center line in the large triangle. Mark the triangles "gray," the center "black and white," and the outside edge "black" on the backs of the foundations.

Place registration marks across the curves and cut the pieces apart.

4. Following the basic crazy-piecing directions (page 54), piece each foundation with the selection of fabric in the marked colors. The foundations are finished size with no seam allowances included, so fabric must extend beyond the edges on all sides and be trimmed to a ¼" seam allowances.

5. Piece the curved block sections together, or if you would prefer, turn the seam allowance of the center curve under and appliqué it between the black edges. Measure carefully to ensure the blocks measure 7½" when they are completed.

6. Join the corner sections together in the same way, by piecing or appliqué. Following the quilt layout diagram, assemble the top (Fig. 3–8). Staystitch around the edge in

Fig. 3–8. CRAZY CRACKER layout.

the seam allowance with a small stitch before removing the foundations.

7. Cover the cable cord with the 1½" black solid, bias fabric trimmed to a ¼" seam allowance. Follow the directions for TAKE TWO I , page 19, to complete the piped edge and prepare for quilting.

8. The quilt in the photo was machine quilted with silver metallic thread, following the illustration in Fig. 6–3 in Chapter 6, page 138.

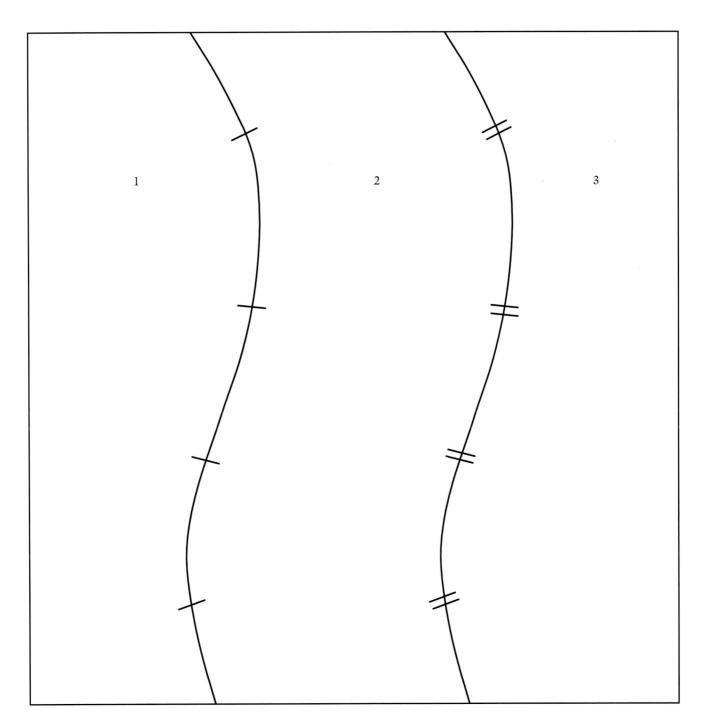

Full-sized CRAZY CRACKER block pattern.

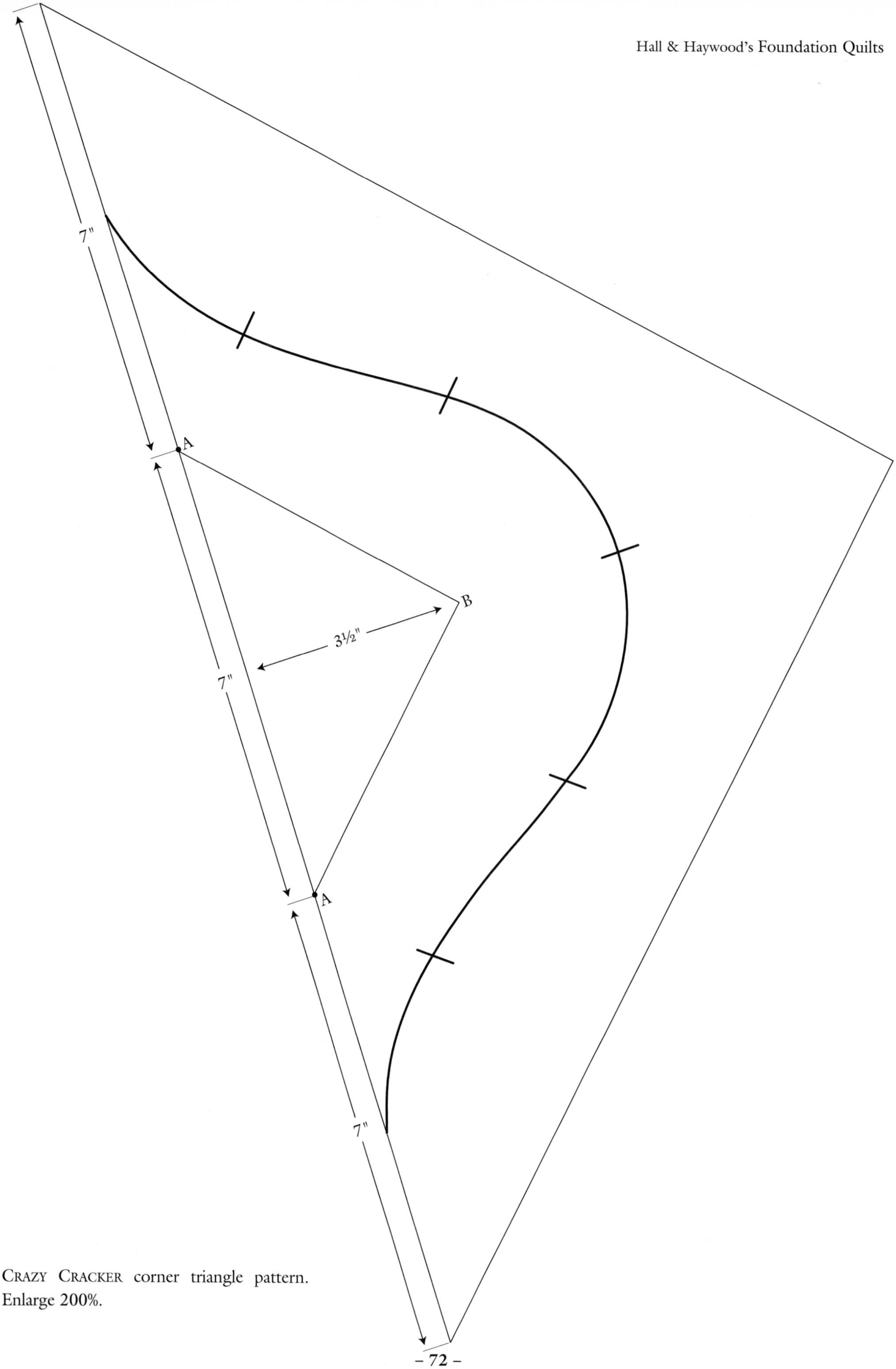

7"

A

7"

B

3½"

7"

A

7"

CRAZY CRACKER corner triangle pattern.
Enlarge 200%.

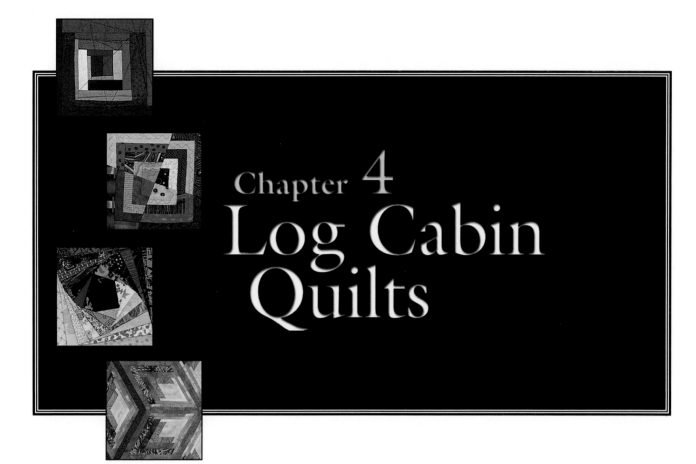

Chapter 4
Log Cabin Quilts

Log Cabin designs are among the most popular of all quilt patterns. Simple to construct, easily made with scraps or planned yardage, and dynamic in graphics, they appeal to beginning and advanced quiltmakers alike. There is something in this design that brings us back time and time again, to try a different arrangement of colors, a new variation of patterning, or a completely innovative approach to placing strips around a center square.

Log Cabin quilts have been recorded in the British Isles as far back as 1650, Averil Colby, cites that date for a square English perfume bag, worked in lat-

ticed silks. Documented British Log Cabin quilts have been found dating from the second quarter of the nineteenth century. There are several interesting theories attempting to explain the origins of the design, none of which can be verified.

In the British Isles, the pattern has been called "Canadian Logwork" and "Egyptian" or "Mummy pattern." When the tombs in Egypt were opened in the nineteenth century, thousands of small animal mummies were found and shipped back to England. Initially regarded as curiosities, ultimately they were distributed to farms for fertilizer. The British Museum collections include small mummified cats and birds, wrapped in perfect Log Cabin patterns, some even with light and dark colored diagonal planes dividing the blocks. These designs were accessible and potentially familiar to the general population.

The French as well as the British were caught up in the Egyptian craze. In *Quilter's Newsletter Magazine #293*, Darcy Pattison cites "Description de l'Egypte," which is a document published by French scholars who went to Egypt with Napoleon. It contains pictures of mummies and the Log Cabin design. She states, "It seems clear that this design source was available as early as 1821." It is reasonable to think that the patterning could have been an inspiration for Log Cabin designs, both in continental Europe and Great Britain during the nineteenth century.

Another intriguing theory about the pattern has to do with the way land was cultivated in Britain, Scandinavia, and other parts of Europe. Communal tenancy farming was widespread, and the fields were arranged in strips called "run-rigs," allowing for both infields and outfields of differing arability and productivity. Every farmer was allotted an equal portion of wet and dry fields. Early maps of run-rig farming show fields laid out in blocks of parallel strips running at right angles to each other, a perfect Log Cabin design. One

could conjecture that the light and dark sides represent the dry and the wet fields. Janet Rae, author of *The Quilts of the British Isles*, believes it is entirely appropriate to go to the land for patterns.

A third possibility involves the Isle of Man, which claims the Log Cabin quilt as its own. It is called the "roof" pattern there and was pieced either from mixed scraps of old fabric or in a traditional red-and-white zigzag design. Manx quilters developed their own method of working, using the size of their hands, fingers, and thumbs for measuring. Fabric is torn, and the strips are stitched on the foundation and then folded along their length, forming pleated logs.

Gill Turley teaches the Manx method in Britain and mainland Europe, preserving the technique, which has been handed down by word of mouth. She says, "Having once dismissed the method as being haphazard and inaccurate, I suddenly began to enjoy the freedom of measuring the fabrics against my hand, tearing the strips, and hand sewing. To me, there no longer seemed a great need for my earlier love of speed and precision in quiltmaking, and I began to appreciate the sheer joy of handling the fabric, picking up the colors and putting them into the quilt blocks."

Gill's Manannan's Cloak is a wonderful example of a quilt made by using this unique

technique, and at the same time incorporating Manx folklore (Photo 4–1). Manannan was a Celtic sea god who had the power to protect the Isle from danger. Time and time again, he would envelope the island with a veil of mist to hide its beauty and protect it from invaders, particularly English royalty. To this day on the island, the sea mist is still known as "Manannan's Cloak." The lovely soft colors of Gill's quilt evoke just that misty feeling. After she visited the Isle of Man, she made her Log Cabin quilt in the traditional style by using her hand as the measurement for the center blocks. When she decided to make an inner border of small blocks, she enlisted the hand of a neighboring child for size. The outer corners of the quilt are strip pieced on foundations. See pages 78–79 for THE ISLE OF MAN ROOF pattern by Joan Thrussell.

Photo 4–1

detail

full quilt on page 80

In the United States, we have long thought the Log Cabin pattern to be the one intrinsically American design. We speak of the red hearth and the sunny and shady sides of the house. It fit well into our history at a time when we were moving west in wagons, building log homes and new lives. In fact, the Log Cabin design may well have been brought here by our forebears, either from Britain, Canada, or Scandinavia. It may ultimately turn out to be an evolution of a design idea in several parts of the world almost simultaneously. Given the predilection of quilters to find useable patterns and designs in everyday settings, together with the paucity of confirmed data and dates for these quilts, it is so far only a matter for intriguing speculation.

The earliest dated American Log Cabin quilt found in any of the state quilt searches was made in 1869. Whatever its origins, the pattern was immediately and immensely popular, constructed in cotton, wools and later, silks. Given the different weights and types of fabrics available for quilt-making and used for strips, this pattern was a natural one to be pieced on a foundation. These foundations were usually waste fabrics, leftovers from household sewing, and quite often were heavy. The quilts were usually tied. The lack of quilting on these early Log Cabin quilts can most likely be attributed to the fact that quilting can be difficult through a fabric foundation.

The classic Log Cabin pattern begins with a center square, often of red, sometimes of black, surrounded on two sides by light value strips, and on the remaining sides by dark strips. The block is thus divided into light and dark halves along one diagonal. The blocks can be arranged to create many different designs, some named and well-known, others unique and quite inventive.

A Log Cabin top from Jane's collection is a classic design made in the last quarter of the nineteenth century from cotton fabrics hand stitched to several different heavy foundation fabrics (Photo 4–2). The blocks have been sewn together in a Barn-Raising design, a series of alternating light and dark, ever-expanding diamond rings. It is an unfinished top, which allows us to see the hand construction and the varied foundation materials.

Photo 4–2

detail

full quilt on page 80

Jane found a wonderful wool Log Cabin top at an antique show (Photo 4–3). The blocks are arranged in a Straight-Furrow configuration. Alternate rows on both planes are darker than the adjacent fabrics, creating a strong secondary pattern commonly termed "zebra striped." Note the excellent diagonal "piano-key" border, also sewn on a fabric foundation.

Instead of a diagonal division of light and dark values, the strips for a Log Cabin can be arranged alternately around the

Photo 4–3

detail

full quilt on page 80

center, first light, then dark, to create the Courthouse Steps variation with tessellating hourglass figures in both values. When multiple blocks are joined, balls of color resembling Japanese lanterns are formed. This was a very popular variation of the Log Cabin design, done in cottons, wools, and silks at the turn of the century. Kathlyn Sullivan's wool challis and silk Courthouse Steps quilt top has skillful arrangements of soft colors, creating Japanese lantern designs in the body of the quilt, with sharper contrasting colors in the borders (Photo 4–4). The coloration of this graphic design creates a southwestern-like palette.

Photo 4–4

detail

full quilt on page 81

Barbara Goebel's STEPPING UP TO PLAIDS is a Courthouse Steps Log Cabin quilt, in plaid fabrics, with a fresh contemporary look (Photo 4–5). Use of the same fabrics in a string border continues her approach of using traditional design elements and fabrics that ordinarily announce "country" to stretch beyond both the traditional and the country looks.

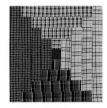

Photo 4–5

larger photo on page 81

Given the Log Cabin's popularity and its ease of construction, it wasn't long before the basic graphics were altered in color, shape, and focus. Jane's antique Log Cabin variation, sometimes called "White House Steps," contains light and dark fabrics not placed in any traditional order (Photo 4–6). Rather, concentric boxes are created, with successive rows of the same color pieced around all four sides. The rows alternate light and dark values.

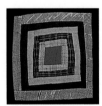

Photo 4–6

full quilt on page 81

FRACTURED STEPS, Kathlyn Sullivan's project (page 89), uses somewhat the same arrangement of color and value. However, her finished blocks are cut up into measured segments, which are re-combined, creating interesting color combinations and transparency effects.

Eileen Gudmundson's Amish Log Cabin project, DEEP PURPLE

HAZE (page 86) contains random strips, randomly assembled. The wide, narrow, and uneven strips give an entirely different air to the traditional pattern. There is no attempt to control strip size or color. It is easily worked and stabilized on foundations, so even though they appear skewed, the blocks fit together precisely.

In contrast, Lynne Harrill's SUBURBAN NIGHTS is a random Log Cabin quilt with colors and fabrics arranged consistently in each block to give a contemporary look with a center focus (Photo 4–7). The cleverly built-in border suggests a classic Log Cabin with its diagonal light-dark arrangement.

Photo 4–7

full quilt on page 81

Totally changing the focus of the Log Cabin block, Barbara Kaempfer's project (page 93) is a twisted Log Cabin design. By tipping the center square and controlling the colors of the strips as they are sewn on the newly angled planes, she creates a ribbon effect twisting across the face of the quilt. As with the classic Log Cabin, the blocks can be rotated and joined to form different layouts.

Barbara's COLORWHEEL 2 (Photo 4–8) is a more complicated twist in a swirling design

built of hexagons and equilateral triangles. The twisted Log Cabin can be done in almost any shape, which gives infinite possibilities for more twists and new designs. The quilt was made of pointillist fabrics with light to dark value gradations, and it is framed.

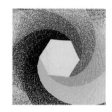

Photo 4–8

full quilt on page 82

RAINFOREST, Eileen Sullivan's project (page 97) has an off-center Log Cabin on diamond foundations. Moving the beginning patch away from the center changes the graphics of the design completely. She has positioned the colors and values to create an exciting six-pointed star.

Eileen has made a number of off-center Log Cabin designs, and her rectangular piece, BLUE OVAL STUDY, has narrow logs on three sides of the center square and wide logs on only one side (Photo 4–9). The resulting block grows faster in one direction, becoming a rectangle rather than a square (Fig. 4–1). Each block creates one-quarter of an

Photo 4–9

full quilt on page 82

oval, and a complete oval requires two blocks and two mirror-image blocks, because the shape of the blocks makes rotation impossible.

Flavin Glover has long used Log Cabin designs to make scenic quilts but usually has worked without foundations. She did use them, however, in BORNEO FARM-SCAPES (Photo 4–10). Inspired by the steep vertically plowed rows and furrows seen on the mountainsides in Malaysia, she was challenged to re-create this image in a Log Cabin landscape quilt, which required triangular blocks as well as square and rectangular blocks.

Photo 4–10

detail

full quilt on page 82

Flavin says, "Foundation piecing enabled me to subdivide the vertical fields into random-shaped blocks. Initially, I marked logs on the paper foundations, but realized I had to be less rigid if the goal was to randomly piece logs of varying widths in a less organized manner. While some people piece on foundations for precision, I needed them for stability and control of the block shapes when I joined the haphazardly shaped blocks into units. It worked! The quilt is smooth and flat. Hand quilting emphasizes the activity and growth within some of the fields and highlights the fabric motifs and log shapes in others."

AUTUMN IN BURGUNDY I, II, AND III is a miniature silk Log Cabin made by Sonja Shogren (Photo 4–11). The elegant triptych contains classic blocks arranged in an abstract composition. It was made after Sonja returned home from a visit to France. In addition to the striking value contrasts, the texture of the tiny 1½" blocks results in a faceted, jewel-like surface in the background areas. Sonja works only with tiny blocks, in both traditional and innovative designs.

Photo 4–11

detail

full quilt on page 83

In the twentieth century, with the growth of quiltmaking, the wide use of sewing machines, and easy access to fabric, Log Cabin quilts began to be made without foundations. Quilters could and did stitch blocks quickly, and because it was so easy to construct, the pattern became one of the most widely used. The strips were sometimes not cut quite evenly, and ¼" seams were often sewn less than perfectly. As a result, the pattern was skewed because outside strips often had to be trimmed or extended so the blocks would fit together. With the return to popularity of foundation work, quilters are also returning to the use of foundations for accurate Log Cabin blocks. Consistent block size, control of logs against stretching, and complex designs make this extra step valid.

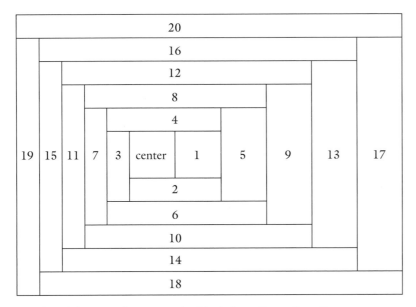

Fig. 4–1. Diagram of a rectangular block from BLUE OVAL STUDY.

THE ISLE OF MAN ROOF PATTERN

by Joan Thrussell

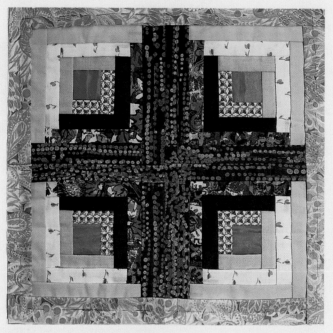

Four Manx Log Cabin blocks.

Log Cabin patchwork has been made since the early part of the nineteenth century on the Isle of Man. Fabric was recycled from clothing, old curtains, and scraps of all kinds. The blocks were pieced with the traditional light and dark diagonal halves. These quilts were economical, quick, and easy to make and are still being made today.

With an isolated, rural population and few tools, the Manx quilters devised their own method of constructing the Log Cabin pattern. They used the span of the hand for the size of the foundation, the length of the inside of the thumb to the base of the thumbnail for the strip width, and the inside length of the middle finger as the size for the center squares. Some say that the width of the little fingernail should be used as the seam allowance measurement. All the pieces of fabric were torn, initially cut with a knife or by biting. The original work would have been by lamp or candlelight, which is probably why big stitches were used. The pleat in the work hides these nicely as well as giving extra warmth. There is no batting or backing. The fronts and backs of the blocks are attached to each other separately.

Block Construction

✳ For the foundation, add ½" to the measurement of the span of your hand as a seam allowance. The center square is the inside length of your middle finger. Fold the fabrics twice, and pinch the points to find the centers. Sometimes the center square is a special piece of fabric, such as silk, satin, or a fancy print instead of the bright "fireside" square.

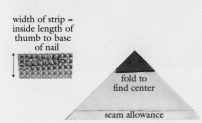

width of strip = inside length of thumb to base of nail

fold to find center

seam allowance

✳ Hand stitch with a running stitch. Stop and backstitch when you reach ¼" from the end of the square and put the needle through to the back. Leave the thread dangling, ready to begin stitching the next strip. To keep the needle threaded, you may want to use doubled thread.

inside length of middle finger

span of hand

seam allowance

✳ Make a lengthwise fold in the strip just stitched, folding back two-thirds of the fabric. Pin it in place and add a second strip of the same fabric. Bring the needle and thread to the front side at the point where you stopped stitching the first strip. This point will not be at the beginning of the second strip, but you should catch the fold of the first strip. The unsewn ½" will be secured by the next round of stitching.

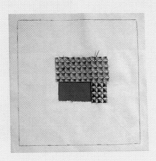

✳ The pattern is arranged traditionally, with two light strips followed by two dark strips in each row. Continue stitching, folding, rotating the block, and stitching again, using one continuous thread. Leave ¼" free around the edge of the foundation, and baste around the finished block ½" from the edge of the strips. Note: Only four pins are needed for adding the strips. Place them at an angle across each corner, removing and re-using them in order.

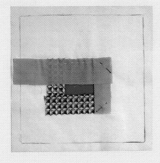

✳ Fold back the foundations, match the raw edges of the strips only, and stitch the front sides of the blocks together with a backstitch.

pin back

pin back

Backstitch right sides together.

trim edges and baste about ½"

✳ Working from the back, turn under one raw edge and join the foundations with "run and fell" (a hemming stitch).

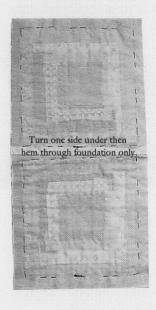

Turn one side under then hem through foundation only.

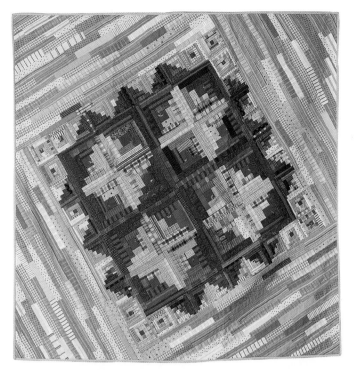

Photo 4–1. (TOP) MANANNAN'S CLOAK, 47½" x 47½", 1996. Made by Gill Turley.

Photo 4–3. (BOTTOM) Antique wool zebra-striped Log Cabin, 74" x 82", circa 1895. Maker unknown. From the collection of Jane Hall.

Photo 4–2a. (TOP) Antique classic Log Cabin top, 56" x 56", circa 1885. Maker unknown. From the collection of Jane Hall.

Photo 4–2b. (BOTTOM) Antique classic Log Cabin back (detail), showing varied foundations.

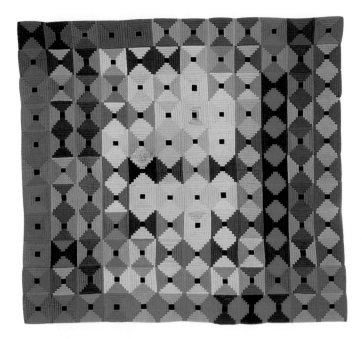

Photo 4–4. Antique wool challis Courthouse Steps Log Cabin top, 56" x 52", circa 1870. Maker unknown. From the collection of Kathlyn Sullivan.

Photo 4–5. STEPPING UP TO PLAIDS, detail, 82" x 100", 2000. Made by Barbara Goebel from a design by Judie Rothermel.

Photo 4–6. (LEFT) Antique White House Steps Log Cabin quilt, 47" x 65", circa 1890. Maker unknown. From the collection of Jane Hall.

Photo 4–7. (RIGHT) SUBURBAN NIGHTS, 43" x 43", 1998. Made by Lynne G. Harrill.

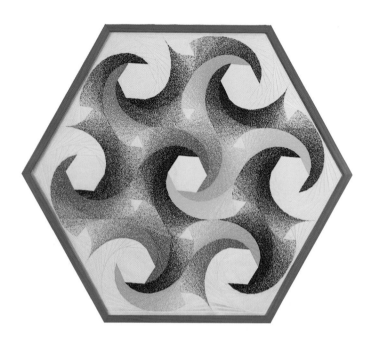

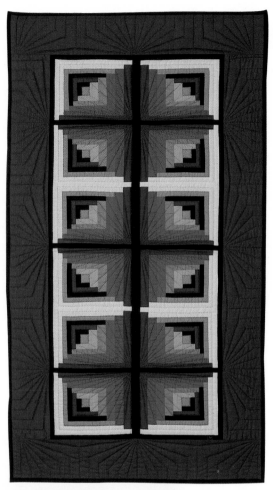

Photo 4–8. (TOP) COLORWHEEL 2, 23" x 26", 1996. Made by Barbara T. Kaempfer.

Photo 4–9. (RIGHT) BLUE OVAL STUDY, 27" x 49", 1983. Made by Eileen Sullivan.

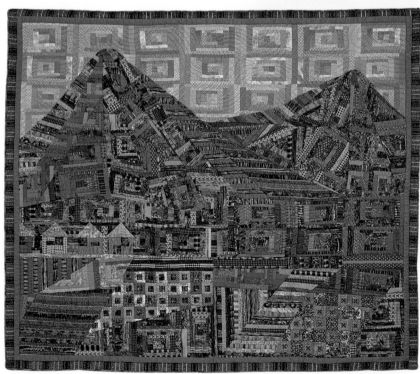

Photo 4–10. BORNEO FARMSCAPES, 70" x 60", 1999. Made by Flavin Glover.

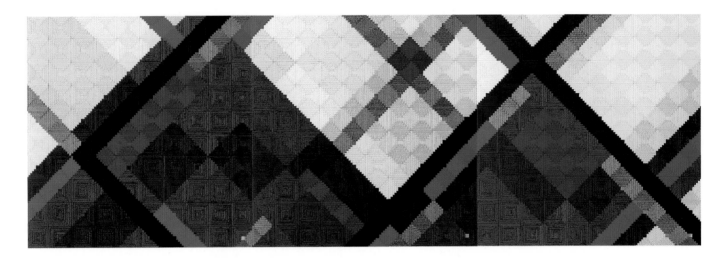

Photo 4–11a. Autumn in Burgundy I, II, and III, 20" x 20" (each piece), 1994. Made by Sonja C. Shogren.

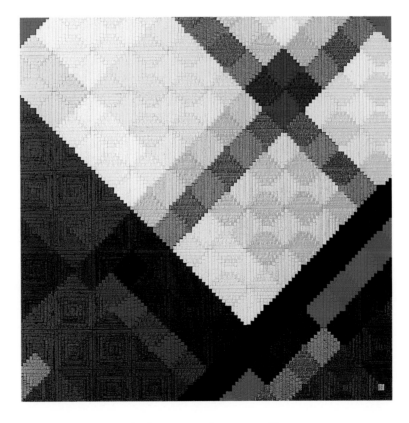

Photo 4–11b. Autumn in Burgundy II.

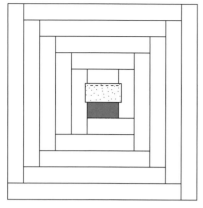

a.

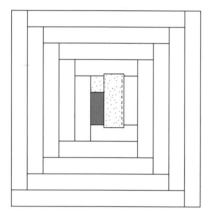

b.

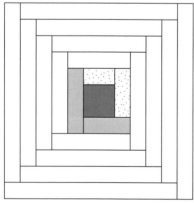

c.

Fig. 4–2. Log Cabin block piecing progression. a. Strip 1 sewn on center square. b. Strip 2 added. c. First row completed.

LOG CABIN PROJECTS

The projects that follow will give you new ways to look at and use this versatile pattern, whether you work traditionally or innovatively. All were pieced with the sewing machine, although handwork is, as always, an option.

The basic Log Cabin block is a simple design, easily executed. In multiples, with the blocks turned in various degrees, the number of arrangements is virtually infinite. We begin with the pattern and directions for the basic block to refresh and hone your Log Cabin skills.

This block can be most accurately pieced by using under pressed-piecing. For a more predominantly dark block, begin piecing with the light value; reverse for a lighter block.

Block Construction

1. Trace the pattern on tracing paper, lightweight interfacing, or fabric.
2. Cut a 1½" center square. Cut two strips an ample 1" wide across the width of both the light and dark fabrics.
3. Pin the center square on the unmarked side of the foundation, right side up, covering the center square with a ¼" seam allowance on all sides.

4. Using under pressed-piecing (see Appendix, page 147), follow the numbered piecing order on the pattern. Sew strip 1 on the first side of the square (Fig. 4–2a). Open it out, press, and trim any excess fabric to ¼" seam allowance. Position strip 2 along the next side of the square and across the end of strip 1 and stitch (Fig. 4–2b). Open, press, and trim as before. Strips 1 and 2 will be light, 3 and 4 will be dark (Fig. 4–2c).

5. Continue piecing successive rows, maintaining the division of light and dark values.

Be sure to turn the block in the same direction with each addition. If you get lost and don't know which strip to sew next, look for the shortest strip. It will be the first strip in each two-step color row.

A larger block can be made by adding another row or two of strips rather than by increasing the width of the strips. Narrow strips create a subtle color span, in contrast to the clunky stair-steps formed by wide strips.

If you want to make a small project of this design, make four blocks and rotate them each 90° to produce a square on point or Sunshine and Shadow set.

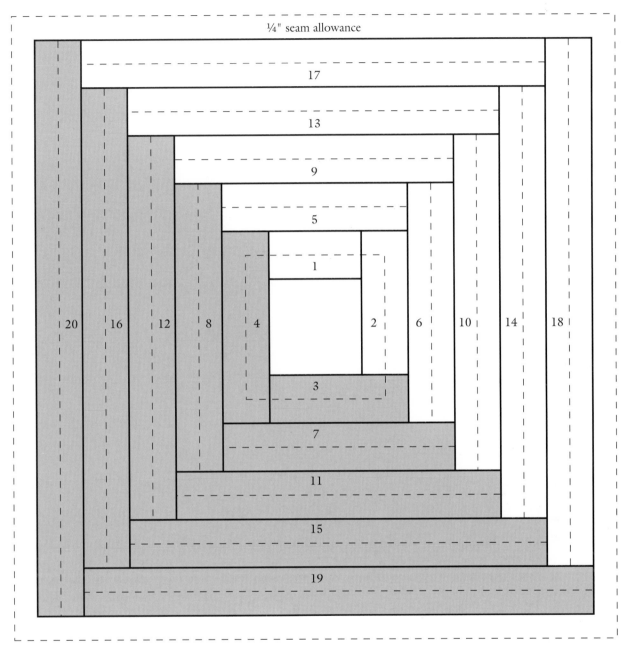

6" finished-size Log Cabin block with 1" center and ½" logs.

LOG CABIN VARIATIONS

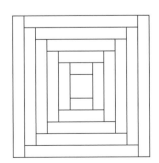

Courthouse Steps

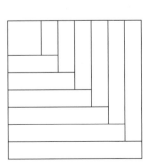

Corner Log Cabin

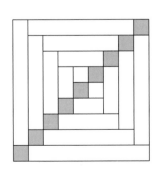

Chimneys and Cornerstones

Deep Purple Haze

Photo 4–12. DEEP PURPLE HAZE, 64½" x 64½". Made by Eileen Gudmundson.

The Log Cabin pattern becomes a showcase for color inspired by Amish quilts, in which free-form piecing was used to create sophisticated complexity. Piecing a Log Cabin block with complete freedom of color placement, strip size, and even piecing progression is not only great fun but also generates creative surprises. This process can lead to quilts with very different looks, depending on color, set, and border choices. Bet you can't make just one! For another version of this design, see Photo 6–1, page 137.

TECHNIQUE:
Random Top Pressed-Piecing

SIZE:
64½" x 64½"

BLOCKS:
Sixteen 8" (finished) blocks

BORDERS:
1½" (finished) sashing and cornerstones
4" (finished) inner border
10" (finished) outer border

MATERIALS:
Blocks – approximately 3 yards total of various fabrics, some in very small amounts

Outer border – 2 yards

Inner border, sashing, cornerstones – 2 yards coordinating but contrasting hues

Backing – 4 yards

Binding – ¾ yard of different hue

Batting

Lightweight paper for foundations

Usual sewing supplies

The fabric should be 100% cotton in solid colors and mostly medium and dark values. Select a lot of colors and use many shades of the same color. Include small amounts of your border and binding fabrics in the blocks to tie the areas of color together. Be aware, however, that with this free-spirited method of working, you may ultimately change your choices for the colors of the sashing and border fabrics.

For a truly Amish look, do not include pastels or prints, and use very few brights. Amish color is grayed and somewhat subtle, with a lot of black and navy. Overdyeing with procion dye in several shades of gray will help if you can't find sufficient fabric in the right colors. In addition, chambrays, twills, sateens, and hand-dyed fabrics can add richness to your palette.

Construction

1. Cut 16 foundations 8½" square.
2. Cut strips randomly with a lot of variety. For instance, a log can be 2" at one end and taper to ½" at the other end. Sort by lengths into piles near your sewing machine, to help you find the right strip as you stitch. Before you cut strips from the border fabric, cut the borders along the fabric length to avoid having to piece them.
3. The blocks centers can and should vary in size, shape, and color, but should be proportional to the block size. For pizazz, pre-piece a multi-patch for some of the centers.
4. Follow the random top pressed-piecing directions in the Appendix, page 145. Piece the logs around the center, using color and width variations in each block, with many narrow logs. Don't worry about one side being light and one dark, as in traditional Log Cabin blocks. Don't even worry about circling the blocks in the same direction. Eileen works freehand, without any preconceived or regulated shapes, cutting and sewing the color at hand, generally working on several blocks at one time. It is her deliberate placement of low-key color and varied values that makes her quilt sing.
5. True the blocks to 8½" and arrange them. It is possible to push the multicolor blocks toward one color or another by

the use of sashing or borders. If any of your preliminary fabric choices for them seem wrong, trust the quilt and your eye and switch fabrics.

6. Cut 24 strips of sashing 2" x 8½". Cut nine 2" square cornerstones.

7. Assemble the quilt. Add borders, butting the corners, as shown in the layout diagram (Fig. 4–3).

8. Layer and baste. Use overall patterns for quilting, such as fans, circles, or grids with straight lines in the body of the quilt. Use different cable patterns in each border.

Add a binding of a different color. The Amish used wide bindings. An inch wide finished size was not unusual.

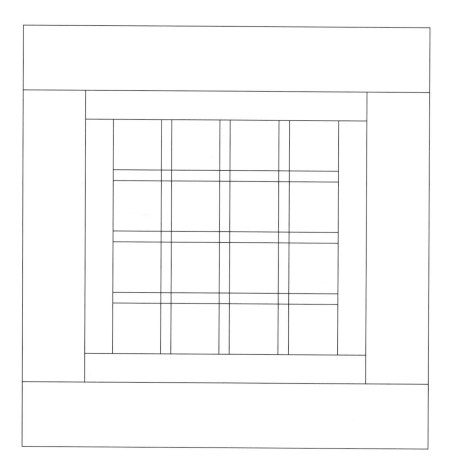

Fig. 4–3. DEEP PURPLE HAZE layout.

Fractured Steps

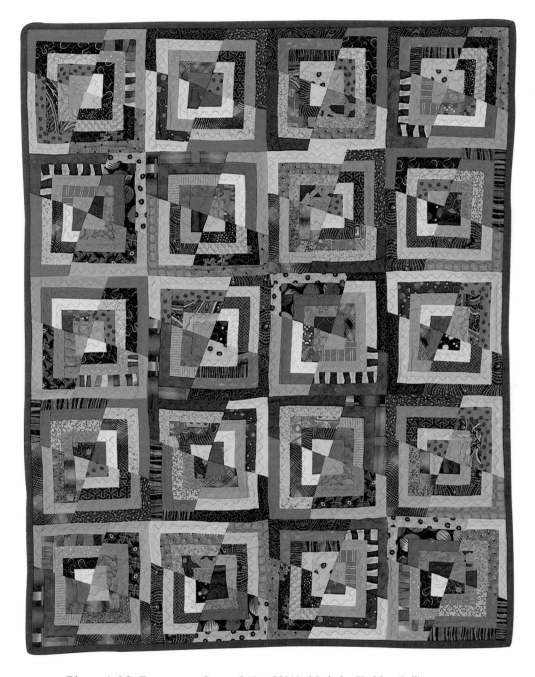

Photo 4–13. FRACTURED STEPS, 26" x 32½". Made by Kathlyn Sullivan.

This is an adaptation of the basic White House Steps pattern in which all the strips in one row are made from the same fabric, which will form concentric squares in each block. The fractured look is achieved by cutting up each pieced block, mixing the segments, and sewing units from four different blocks together to create new ones. Made with bright cotton fabrics, both solid and printed, it is a great way to use leftover strips from other projects. It is a free-wheeling, forgiving design, and it is meant to be fun. With the 20 blocks in this project, there is enough fabric variety to make it visually interesting. The more blocks, the better. The blocks are 7", to take advantage of computer-generated and printed foundations, although the pattern is adaptable to any size block.

Photo 4–13

detail

full quilt on page 89

TECHNIQUE:
Under Pressed-Piecing

SIZE:
26" x 32½"

BLOCKS:
Cut twenty 7" blocks, which will be cut and resewn into 6½" finished units

MATERIALS:
Assorted cotton fabrics, lights and darks, brights, up to 3 yards total

Backing and binding fabric – 1 yard dark fabric

Foundation material – paper or lightweight interfacing

Cotton batting

Usual sewing supplies

Construction

1. Prepare 20 foundations by tracing or needle punching the pattern, see Appendix page 148. If you have a computer, the block is easily drawn and printed on foundations. For this quilt, a computer block design program was used to draw the 7" finished-size pattern (page 92). The block was drawn on a 24 x 24 grid, with each strip represented by two grid units, creating a block with four logs and a large center square.

2. Cut fabric strips 1¼" wide. Cut center squares 3".

3. The blocks are sewn with all four strips in one row made of the same fabric. With value changes between rows, a series of concentric squares is formed. Each block is colored differently. Use the Courthouse Steps progression of stitching two same-sized strips on opposite sides of the center square. Begin by pinning the center square over the drawn lines on the unmarked side of the foundation. Piece the first strip along opposite sides 1 and 2 of the center square and stitch following the under pressed-piecing directions in the Appendix (page 147). Add the same fabric along sides 3 and 4 of the center. The strips are cut with an ample measurement and may extend too far over the next line of stitching. Check and trim if necessary to a ¼" seam allowance. (See Appendix, page 144.)

4. Continue piecing the rows, following the same order. On roughly half the blocks, start with a light center. On the other half, begin with dark. Alternate light and dark fabrics for each row. The strips in the final row should extend over the foundation at least ¼" on all sides.

5. Press the blocks and trim any excess fabric to a ¼" seam allowance beyond the foundations. Staystitch with a small stitch in the seam allowance.

6. Measure and mark 2⅜" in from the left corner of each side (Fig. 4–4). Align your ruler with the marks on opposite sides of the block and make two diagonal cuts across each block. Note: The cutting concept is to divide the side of each block into thirds. While this measurement is not cast in stone, use a consistent measurement to make sure that each block is cut at the same angle so they will fit back together to form identical-sized blocks.

7. Mix up the pieces and sew segments from four different blocks together to create new blocks. Be random in your selection. It is important to sew with an exact ¼" seam allowance. Marked sewing lines may be worthwhile. Square up the blocks if necessary. They should finish at 6½".

8. Arrange the blocks for the most interesting and pleasing color combinations and construct the top (Fig. 4–5). You may find flashes of luminosity and even transparency.

9. If you have used paper foundations, remove them at this point. If you have used interfacing, it may be left in, if you like. Layer, baste, and quilt by machine. The quilt in the photo was machine quilted in a serpentine pattern down the middle of the logs. Bind the raw edges with a narrow, straight-grain binding.

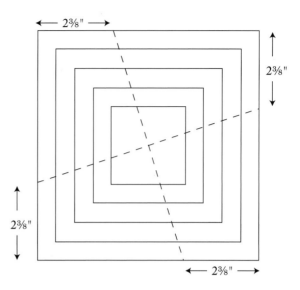

Fig. 4–4. Dividing FRACTURED STEPS blocks.

Fig. 4–5. FRACTURED STEPS layout.

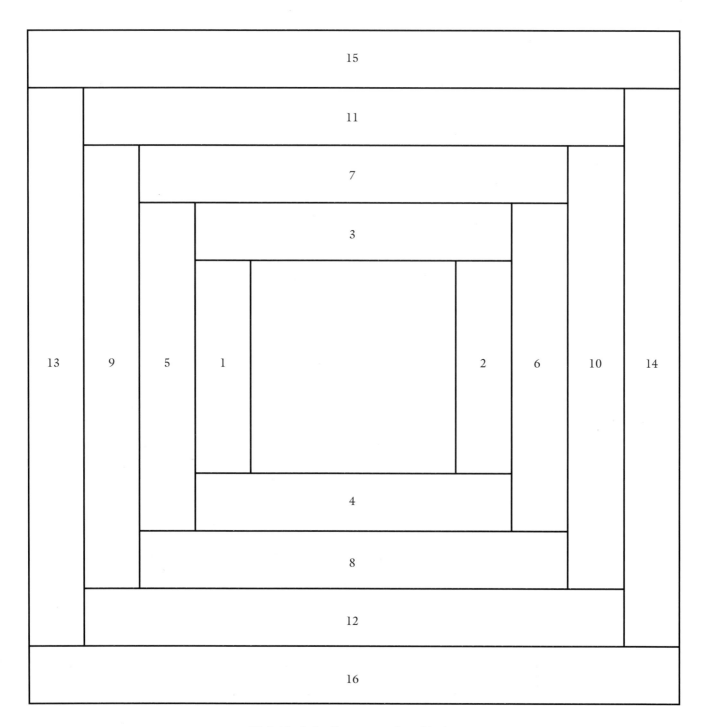

7" finished-size FRACTURED STEP block.

Light and Dark with a Twist

Photo 4–14. LIGHT AND DARK WITH A TWIST, 28" x 28". Made by Barbara T. Kaempfer.

This project gives a new twist to the traditional Log Cabin pattern, creating color in motion. Changing the shape of the logs from strips to triangles completely transforms the graphics of the designs, forming ribbons across the face of the quilt. Barbara has perfected the twisted Log Cabin. She uses many different geometric shapes, giving rise to curved and abstract designs, while she retains the basic feature of the Log Cabin pattern – the infinite possibilities for arrangements of blocks.

Foundations are especially vital to the stability of this version, with its angled cuts and skewed positions. Being able to use the design assistance of writing the color and piecing progressions on the foundations should keep you on the right track. Take a new look at the possibilities as you learn another way to piece this versatile, century-old pattern.

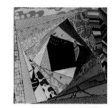

Photo 4–14
detail
full quilt on page 93

TECHNIQUE:
Under Pressed-Piecing

SIZE:
28" x 28"

BLOCKS:
Thirty-six 4" (finished) blocks

BORDERS: 2" (finished)

MATERIALS:
At least 1 yard light value fabrics and 1 yard dark value fabrics in scraps or controlled colors

½ yard black for centers and borders

Backing fabric – 1 yard

Paper for foundations

Batting

Usual sewing supplies

Construction

1. Prepare the foundations by copying the block pattern on page 95, 36 times. See the Appendix, page 147, for options. Keep in mind that, with the twisted Log Cabin design, your finished block will be a mirror image of the marked side of the foundation. Mark the colors or the values on the planes of the pattern (Fig. 4–6a and b). Barbara suggests strongly that you also mark the starting point for each row with an X on the marked side of the foundation (see pattern). All the strips in each row are the same size, and if you lose track of exactly where you are partway through piecing a block, you need to know the location of the beginning of the next row.

2. Cut 1"-wide strips from as many different fabrics as possible, both light and dark val-

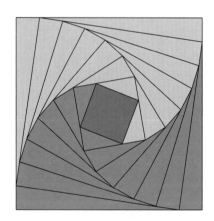

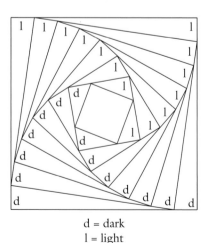

d = dark
l = light

Fig. 4–6. Marking the foundations. a. Value placement. b. Mark values on foundations.

ues. Cut thirty-six 1½" squares of black for the block centers.

3. Pin a center square over the marked square in the center of the block. Start at the side of the center square that you marked with the X, remembering that you must always begin each new row at that comparable point. Position and pin the first light strip along the side of the square, following the basic Log Cabin directions on page 84. Barbara does not pre-cut the strips to size, cutting after the stitching for each "log."

4. Sew *only* from point to point on the marked seam line. Because the design unfolds with no overlapping strips, each strip must be sewn only on the line with no over-stitching. Barbara stitches in place two to three stitches at both the beginning and the end of the line rather than backstitching.

5. After stitching the seam, trim the seam allowance to ⅛", press open the fabric strip and pin it to the foundation.

6. Position the same light value strip for log 2. Stitch as before. Light-value fabric is used for log 1 and log 2, dark value for 3 and 4.

7. For Row 2, it will be necessary to position the fabric strip on the foundation at an angle. Do not match the cut edge of the piece in the first row. From the marked side of the foundation, stab pins at the beginning and end of the stitching line

through the fabric strip to be added. Adjust the strip to the proper angle until the seam allowance is a scant ¼". Stitch, trim the seam allowance, and press open the strip as before. Add a second light strip and two dark strips to complete the row. Continue stitching in rows until the foundation is covered, with the fabric of the final strips extending at least ¼" past the edge of the foundation. Trim excess fabric to a ¼" seam allowance on all sides.

8. Once the 36 blocks have been sewn, play with them and see how many ways you can find to arrange them. All the traditional Log Cabin settings are appropriate for the

twisted Log Cabin. The Barn Raising set used for the quilt in the photo is formed by rotating the blocks quarter- and half-turns to form light and dark squares on point. Stitch the blocks together in pairs and and then in rows. Sew the rows together following the layout (Fig. 4–7, page 96).

9. Attach the borders, butting the corners. Layer and baste. Barbara's quilt is framed, with little or no quilting. If you want to quilt the piece, machine quilting is a good option because of the many seams in the blocks. The quilt also can be tied at the corners of the blocks. Bind the edges with straight-grain binding.

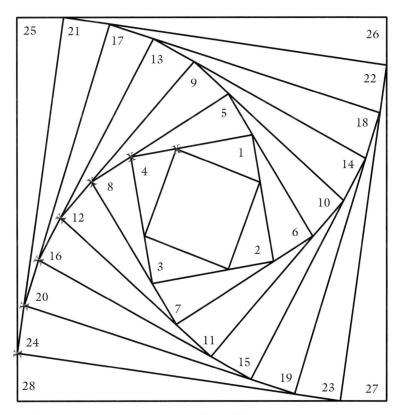

Full-sized LIGHT AND DARK WITH A TWIST block pattern.

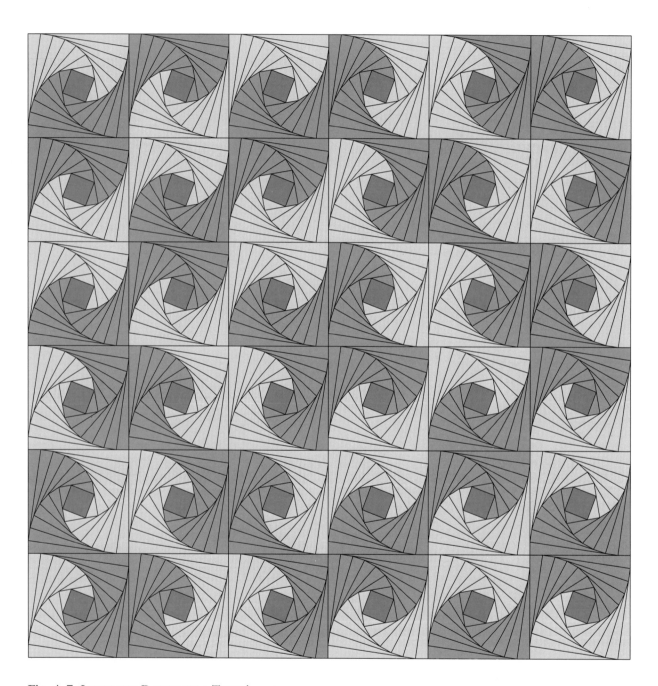

Fig. 4–7. LIGHT AND DARK WITH A TWIST layout.

Rainforest

Photo 4–15. RAINFOREST, 27½" x 32". Made by Eileen Sullivan.

When you move the center of any Log Cabin block to one side, the graphics change drastically. When the basic block is a diamond, the off-centered design bursts into a spectacular six-pointed star. There are two different block arrangements in this quilt, both pieced on the same-sized diamond foundation. In Block 1, thin strips are placed at the top of the design, and wide strips at the bottom. In Block 2, the log width changes from side to side, with thin strips on the right and wide strips on the left. The finished sizes of strips for both blocks are ¼" and ½".

Remembering vacation times in the Caribbean, Eileen chose bright warm colors for this happy piece. She prefers freezer paper for foundations because the fabrics will adhere to it when sewn, flipped, and pressed, eliminating any possibility of shifting.

TECHNIQUE:
Under Pressed-Piecing

SIZE:
27½" x 32" hexagon

BLOCK:
Twelve diamond-shaped blocks, 5½" x 9½" finished (six of Block 1 and six of Block 2)

BORDERS:
¾" inner border (finished)
3½" outer border (finished)

MATERIALS:
Centers – 1¾"-wide strip from a small piece of pale yellow-green

Wide logs – fat quarter, or less, of each of five shades pale aqua to deep turquoise

Thin logs – fat quarter, or less, of each of five shades from pale yellow to coral

Inner border – ⅛ yard, full width of fabric, bright stripe or print in warm tones

Outer border and binding – ¾ yard, full width of fabric, blue-green print

Backing – 1 yard print fabric

Batting

Usual sewing supplies

Cutting Directions

Eileen suggests cutting strips as needed, a few at a time, from the lengthwise grain of the fabric. The inner rows will require less fabric. Cut strips slightly wider than recommended as a safety factor, and trim after sewing as needed before adding the next strip. She cuts the outermost strips for each block generously to be sure there is enough fabric beyond the foundation for the seam allowance.

BLOCKS
Centers: Pale yellow-green
    12 pieces 1¾" x 2¾"
Rows 1 & 2: Pale yellow
    24 pieces ¾" x 2¼"
Rows 3 & 4: Light aqua
    24 pieces 1" x 3"
Rows 5 & 6: Yellow-gold
    24 pieces ¾" x 3"
Rows 7 & 8: Turquoise print
    24 pieces 1" x 4"
Rows 9 & 10: Orange
    24 pieces ¾" x 4"
Rows 11 & 12: Blue-green print
    24 pieces 1" x 4¾"
Rows 13 & 14: Coral
    24 pieces ¾" x 5"
Rows 15 & 16: Bright turquoise
    24 pieces 1" x 5½"
*Rows 17 & 18: Deep coral
    24 pieces ¾" x 6"
*Rows 19 & 20: Deep turquoise
    24 pieces 1" x 7"

Outermost logs: Cut strips very generously to allow enough fabric beyond the foundation.
Inner borders: six strips 1¼" x 14" of bright stripe or print in warm tones, cut from the lengthwise grain if possible.

Outer borders: six strips 4" x 22" of blue-green print, cut from the lengthwise grain if possible.

Construction

1. Make master patterns by tracing the Log Cabin diamonds on pages 100 and 101. Prepare the foundations by needle punching each master pattern on top of a stack of 7–8 sheets of freezer paper, shiny side up, stapled together at the outer edges. (You only need six of each, but we all make mistakes so have few spares!) See needle punching in the Appendix, including the tip for working with freezer paper (page 148).

2. Remove the master patterns and trim each foundation on the outermost lines. These lines are the final stitching lines for joining the blocks. Fabrics need to extend at least ¼" beyond the paper to create the seam allowances.

3. Write color placement on the master pattern and, if necessary, on the individual foundations. The colors are graduated from light to dark in each color family.

4. Assembly-line piece six of the same style of diamonds at one time, as follows: iron the center piece onto each foundation, pre-cut six pieces of fabric for log 1 and chain-piece each foundation in turn. Follow the numbered piecing order on each block.

5. Fold back the foundations on the next sewing line and trim the seam allowance as needed before ironing the logs in place.

6. Continue adding logs until the foundations are covered. Press firmly and trim the fabrics to a ¼" seam allowance beyond the edges of the foundations. Leave the paper in place.

7. Assemble the diamonds in sections, as illustrated (see Fig. 4–9). Remember that when you are setting in pieces, you need to pin, start and stop exactly at the intersection, and back-stitch to hold the seam securely. Add the borders, trimming the ends to the correct angles.

8. Remove the freezer paper after the borders have been added. It is easier to start with the center diamond and remove the foundation logs in order, so that you are pulling with the seam allowance, rather than against it.

9. Layer the quilt top with backing and batting, and baste. Quilt by machine in the ditch between all the wide logs, every other thin log, and on each side of the inner border. Free-motion quilt in the outer border, either in radiating lines or following the fabric designs.

10. Bind the raw edges with a straight-grain binding made from six separate strips, or use a continuous binding with the angles mitered.

Fig. 4–8. RAINFOREST layout, with the two types of blocks outlined in red.

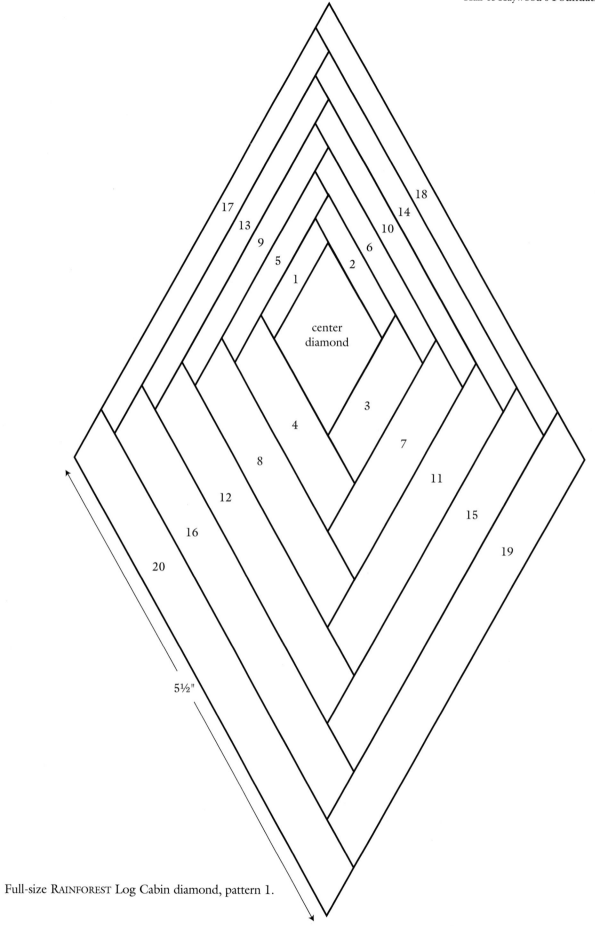

17 13 9 5 1 2 6 10 14 18

center diamond

3 4 7 8 11 12 15 16 19 20

5½"

Full-size RAINFOREST Log Cabin diamond, pattern 1.

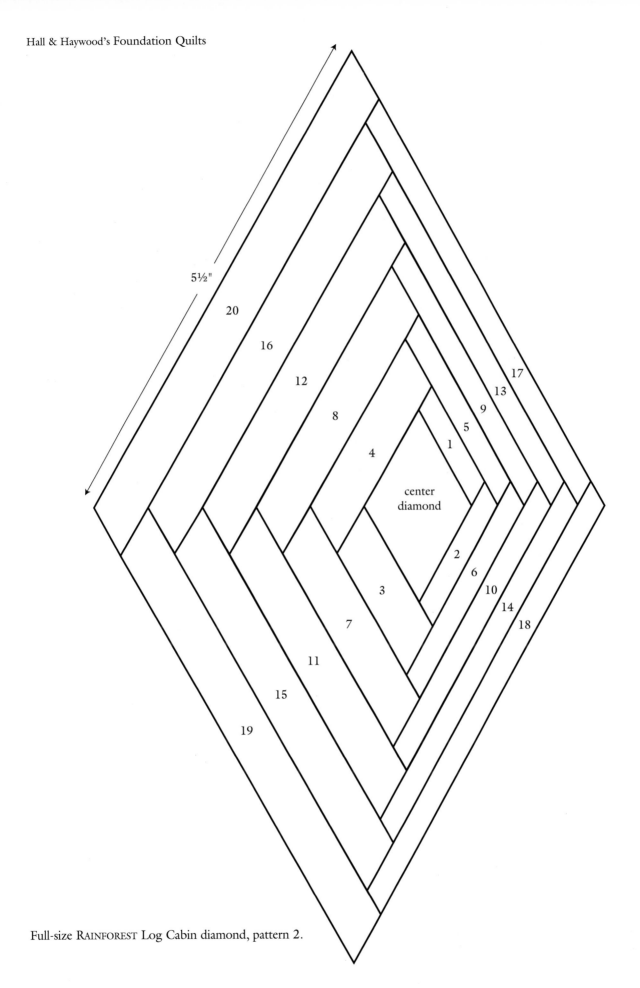

5½"

20

16

12

8

4

1

5

9

13

17

center
diamond

2

6

3

10

14

7

18

11

15

19

Full-size RAINFOREST Log Cabin diamond, pattern 2.

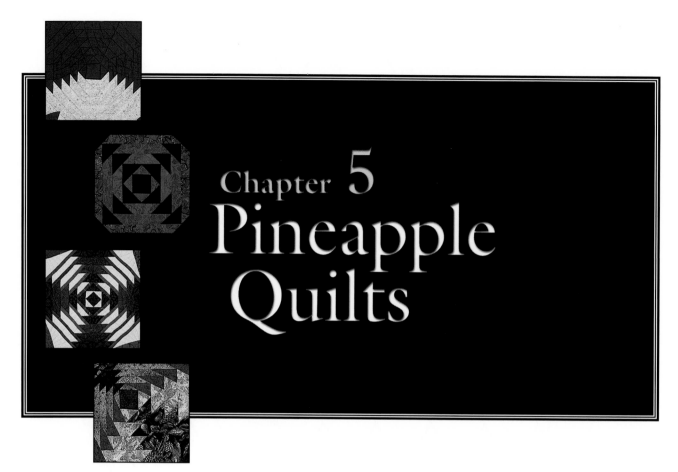

Chapter 5
Pineapple Quilts

The Pineapple pattern is the youngest of our Big Four. Appearing at least 10 years after the earliest Log Cabin quilts, the Pineapple has been considered a "complication" of the Log Cabin by some and is often called the "Pineapple Log Cabin." Other names include Windmill, Windmill Blades, and Maltese Cross.

Once the Log Cabin became a familiar pattern, it was probably only a matter of time before quilters laid extra strips across the diagonal planes to create a new design. Whatever its antecedents, the Pineapple stands on its own as a highly graphic and infinitely variable pattern. While interesting as a single block, this pattern explodes into energy and excitement with multiple blocks. Four blocks are nice, 9 are interesting, but only with 16, 25, and more does this pattern achieve its true potential. "Less is more" does not apply to the Pineapple.

A foundation is essential to achieve stability and piecing precision because the diagonal planes create an inherent instability. With the strips cut on-grain, the diagonal planes create a bias pull that, without a foundation, can stretch as subsequent rows are added. In addition, the large number of seams contribute to another built-in stretch that needs to be controlled.

Like the Log Cabin, Pineapple piecing starts in the center, and proceeds in rows around the center. In a traditional coloration, one value is pieced on the horizontal-vertical plane on four sides of the center, and a contrasting value is sewn on the four diagonal planes of the next row. To understand the piecing progression, you may want to make a sample two-color block from the basic directions that precede the projects in this chapter.

The possibilities for any kind of design with the Pineapple pattern always start with color and its placement on the eight planes of the pattern. Value is more important than a specific color or fabric. The traditional Pineapple coloration results in stars where the diagonal corners of four blocks meet, while the horizontal-vertical planes form a circle around the stars, especially when the value of these planes remains constant. The horizontal-vertical planes may also be seen as windmills or crosses, depending on the values of the fabric used.

Within the traditional parameters of this pattern, there is ample room to create additional graphic interplay. Jane's ULTIMATE PINEAPPLE, made with narrow ⅜" strips, reinterprets an antique wool quilt that all but negates the star and circle effect (Photo 5–1). She used controlled graded colors to focus a light glow around the center of the blocks, and black frames to emphasize

the large red corners of the adjacent blocks. The black windmills stand out strongly against the subtle spans of color of the stars. In order to have complete windmill designs, half and quarter blocks were added at the outer edges of the quilt. The string-pieced piano key border using eight different black fabrics creates a low-key textured frame which is visually lighter than a solid black border would be.

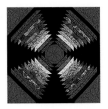

Photo 5–1

full quilt on page 107

The continued fascination with the Pineapple block is that it lends itself to infinite variations. The simplest change is color, which can create entirely new designs without changing the basic piecing progression. As color changes are made, different graphics come into play. Lois Bable's scrap quilt, AND THE EVENING AND THE MORNING WERE THE FIRST DAY, randomly plays with black on the diagonal, forming some stars while only suggesting others (Photo 5–2).

Photo 5–2

full quilt on page 108

The subtle interaction of color and value creates motion, and the ever-changing graphic combinations fascinate the eye.

Jane's exploration of systematic and substantial changes in coloration has resulted in a successful colorwash series. One of them, BERRYPATCH (page 118), is a project for you to try. Adjacent colors from the color wheel are placed diagonally across the face of the quilt on both the stars and on the circles surrounding them, creating a coordinated flow of color.

CHROMA VI: NEBULA is the latest in the series, placing the colorwash in a center-based Barn Raising-type set in which the stars form a series of concentric diamonds (Photo 5–3). There are

Photo 5–3

full quilt on page 108

14 graduated colors in the quilt, beginning with a dark navy in the center star and ending at the outer edges of the quilt with gold. The hand-dyed, sueded cotton fabrics were pieced in small 6" blocks to concentrate the effect of the color fields. The design was planned with color paste-ups, and each block was numbered and shaded before piecing began.

Elizabeth Byrom's DECEMBER contains sets of nine Pineapple

blocks which create multiple units with built-in sashes and borders (Photo 5–4). Each nine-

Photo 5–4

full blocks on page 108

block unit is self-contained with color placements and variations that create a larger overall design, contributing to the unity of the whole quilt. In another use of color to create pattern, ALHAMBRA LEGACY, by Vicki Doolittle, is a dramatic Pineapple medallion quilt (Photo 5–5). She placed colors nontraditionally within the basic block to form an intricate pattern, background, and borders. The subtle and striking balance of the colors within the blocks and the borders is extremely satisfying both visually and intellectually.

Photo 5–5

full quilt on page 108

Allison Lockwood limited herself to two colors in A NEW AGE RED AND WHITE, but used more than 50 each of red and white fabrics (Photo 5–6). She not only changed color placement within the blocks, but combined both 6" and 9" blocks in

what is truly a "blockbuster." She arrived at the final color placement after doing several fabric paste-ups of alternative arrangements, see design possibilites on page 110. Allison says, "While this method might be considered very tedious in our computer age, it works well for me. The slow and methodical process is pleasant and really helps me to understand how the particular block works. I think we sometimes forget how well our 'built-in' computers work!"

Photo 5–6

full quilt on page 109

Pineapple quilts require planning to achieve the desired graphic and color effect. Dixie's TRIPLE PLAY consists of 3", 6", and 9" blocks, with only minor deviations from the traditional coloration in any single block (Photo 5–7). The block composition was graphed out in advance,

Photo 5–7

full quilt on page 111

with the color planned for each individual block. Without having made actual fabric paste-ups, however, it was difficult to pre-

dict how specific fabric choices would work with those in adjacent blocks. As the piecing proceeded, many of the planned choices had to be changed.

Sharon Rexroad uses two differently shaped blocks in her quilt DIAMOND PINEAPPLE #8: THE FAERIE RING (Photo 5–8). She had been working with diamond shaped Pineapples for some time but this quilt was the first time she used both the diamond Pineapple and the traditional square Pineapple blocks together. The diamond blocks create movement and focus. The light and dark value changes provide prominent highlights, and her skillful color placements enhance the multiple secondary designs. According to Sharon, "This actually started as a design study in luminosity." It is highly successful.

Photo 5–8

full quilt on page 111

Within the block, sizes and shapes of strips can be changed. Lengthening the horizontal and vertical strips so that the diagonal strips become same-sized triangles leads to the Flying Geese Pineapple design. An example, is GEESE IN THE CABIN (Photo 5–9), a turn-of-the-century wool quilt found at an antique show by Kate Egerton. The strong black lines of diagonal triangles seem to hover over the field of bright colors. This quilt was the inspiration for the FLYING GEESE PINEAPPLE project on page 121. Jane used 25 different red print fabrics to liven up this two-color quilt, keeping the diagonal overlay of black triangles.

Photo 5–9

full quilt on page 111

Amy Chapman's quilt WAKE UP KATIE! is a strong and interesting interpretation of the Flying Geese Pineapple design, with the same-sized triangles on the horizontal and vertical planes, rather than the more usual diagonal location (Photo 5–10). This configuration creates a straight grid, echoing the block orientation. Her addition of a single block with reversed coloration is inspired.

Photo 5–10

full quilt on page 112

The corners of the Pineapple pattern provide another opportunity for easily made changes to the basic block. In PLEIADES PINEAPPLE, eight-pointed stars were added in the space where

four blocks join (Photo 5–11). It was a simple matter to draft the star blocks to fit the space, omit the corner squares when piecing the block, and piece the stars into the holes at the corners. Half and quarter blocks were added at the outer edges of the quilt so the star designs would be complete.

Photo 5–11

full quilt on page 112

An even easier corner change is the one that forms four-pointed stars in Dixie's GLORY (page 125), one of our Pineapple projects. This simple change is built into the block, and the stars form as the blocks are joined, with no separate piecing. She used the same corner stars in her large quilt, SPACE LIGHTS (Photo 5–12).

Photo 5–12

full quilt on page 113

Dixie has been working on a series that slices one strip into two in one or more planes of the traditional pattern. GLORY (page 125), SPACE LIGHTS, and WEBSITE (Photo 5–13) are made with ¾"-wide diagonal strips, each divided into a ¼" and a ½" strip.

These are pieced separately on the foundation to insure stability and precision, rather than being strip pieced and added as one.

Photo 5–13

full quilt on page 112

In SPACE LIGHTS, the ¼" diagonal strips are the same color as the background formed by the horizontal-vertical strips, lightening the stars and making them appear to float. GLORY's diagonal slices are the same color as the four-pointed star, reinforcing those accents. In WEBSITE, fabric from the final border was used in slices on all eight planes, giving a dimensional effect and eventually culminating in the "webs" that form the first border.

Finally, skewing the Pineapple block to an off-center configuration creates multiple graphic effects. It results in diamond, square, and oval shapes in addition to the usual circles and stars. The strips around the center square become different finished sizes, depending on the proximity of the center to the sides of the block. This structure adds a second variable to the piecing process. In addition to the value change in the fabrics from one plane to another, there is now a change in the width of the strips, often of the same value. Once the process is understood and mas-

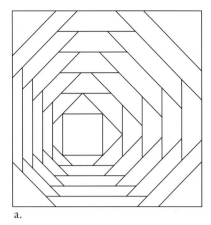

a.

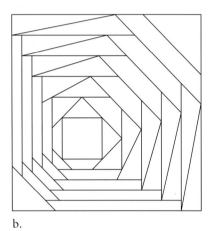

b.

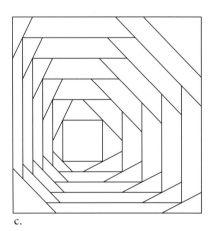

c.

Fig. 5–1. Off-center Pineapple variations a, b, and c.

tered, the resulting design is easily worked and can be exciting.

The angles and positions of the diagonal strips control the graphics in these variations of the off-center Pineapple pattern, and the possibilities are endless. A few common interpretations can be found in Fig. 5–1. In Fig. 5–1a, just as in the classic pattern, the strips in both pairs of diagonal planes are parallel to each other. However, the strips in one corner of the block are exactly half the width of those in the opposing sections, and the remaining pair of diagonal strips measure, roughly, between the width of the other strips.

In the block in Fig. 5–1b, the strips in only one set of diagonal planes are parallel to each other. The strips in the second set of diagonal planes are drawn with one end connecting to the first horizontal or vertical strip in the row. Succeeding rows in each plane are parallel to the first strip; however, the angles of the opposing planes are tipped.

In Fig. 5–1c, the first set of diagonal strips is parallel to the opposite set. The second set of diagonal strips is drafted so that identical triangles are created in each corner of the block. These triangles can have legs of equal or unequal length, depending on the angle of the diagonal line.

SHARDS, the off-center Pineapple project on page 130, has same-size triangles for one set of opposing diagonals, but because they are tipped rather than paral-

lel to each other, the resulting design produces a swooping effect.

In a different off-center pattern, the blocks in Mary Ann Herndon's PINEAPPLE STRETCH are designed with gradated Flying Geese triangles on the diagonal planes, which generate strong wavy lines (Photo 5–14). With the blocks set on point, the resulting optical illusion gives the quilt a three-dimensional effect with a block that is as simple to piece as a traditional Pineapple. Mary Ann used just two hues, in a variety of values, for this eye-stretching quilt.

Photo 5–14

detail

full quilt on page 112

Mary Ann's quilt is just one of many in this chapter that contains a great number of fabrics within a controlled color palette. This approach is different from using either random scraps or just a few fabrics in a specific color scheme. PINEAPPLE STRETCH is limited to two hues of gradually darkening values. PLEIADES PINEAPPLE has a wide variety of blues and white-on-white fabrics, as does GLORY. SPACE LIGHTS has 20 low-contrast black prints to give a twinkle to the background, reinforcing the theme of the quilt. Allison's A NEW AGE RED AND WHITE contains about

(continued on page 114)

Photo 5–1. THE ULTIMATE PINEAPPLE, 76" x 87", 1997. Made by Jane Hall.

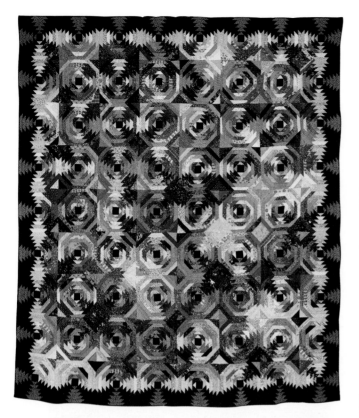

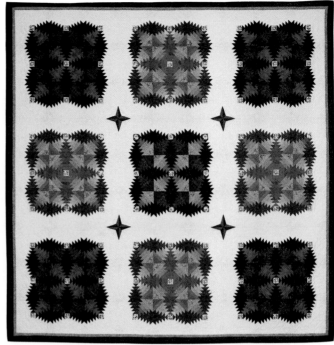

Photo 5–2. (TOP) AND THE EVENING AND THE MORNING WERE THE FIRST DAY, 96" x 108", 1995. Made by Lois M. Bable.

Photo 5–4. (TOP) DECEMBER, 84" x 84", 1996. Made by Elizabeth Byrom.

Photo 5–3. (BOTTOM) CHROMA VI: NEBULA, 58"x 58", 1997. Made by Jane Hall.

Photo 5–5. (BOTTOM) ALHAMBRA LEGACY, 74" x 84", 1998. Made by Victoria Doolittle.

Photo 5–6. A New Age Red and White, 81" x 81", 1997. Made by Allison Lockwood.

Design possibilities for A New Age Red and White

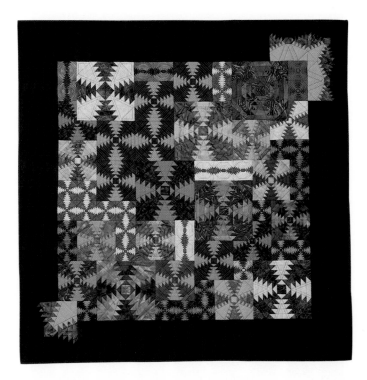

Photo 5–7. TRIPLE PLAY, 49" x 49, 1997. Made by Dixie Haywood.

Photo 5–8. DIAMOND PINEAPPLE #8: THE FAERIE RING, 65" x 65", 1998. Made by Sharon Rexroad.

Photo 5–9. GEESE IN THE CABIN, 68" x 75", circa 1900. Maker unknown. From the collection of Katherine E. Egerton.

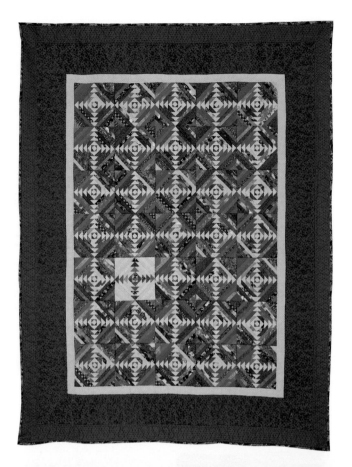

Photo 5–10. (TOP) WAKE UP KATIE!, 80" x 100", 1999. Designed by Amy and Katie Chapman and made by Amy Chapman.

Photo 5–13. (BOTTOM) WEBSITE, 53" x 53", 1997. Made by Dixie Haywood.

Photo 5–11. (TOP) PLEIADES PINEAPPLE, 82" x 92", 1996. Made by Jane Hall and Dixie Haywood for the quilt raffle at the International Quilt Festival in Houston, Texas. From the collection of Mary Underhill.

Photo 5–14. (BOTTOM) PINEAPPLE STRETCH, 72" x 72", 1998. Made by Mary Ann Herndon.

Photo 5–12. SPACE LIGHTS, 84" x 102", 2000. Made by Dixie Haywood.

(continued from page 106) 50 each of different red and white fabrics. The Ultimate Pineapple blends more than 75 prints, many of them plaids and replicas of nineteenth-century fabrics. No two blocks are alike. The Flying Geese Pineapple project has 25 same-value red prints, many in the same shade. All these quilts are richer and more interesting because the many fabrics within a given color parameter are blended skillfully.

Borders can easily be built into Pineapple quilts in several ways. By piecing a portion of the final outer blocks with a background fabric, a star image can be completed in the body of the quilt with a solid-appearing border having the texture of a pieced block. The inner borders of WEBSITE, NEBULA, GLORY, and BERRYPATCH were made with this approach. DECEMBER was created with both built-in sashing as well as borders. A partial or complete block pieced with a high contrast, a different color configuration, or even different shapes, makes a successful frame with a special affinity for the design of the quilt. This concept was used to make spectacular borders for A NEW AGE RED AND WHITE, ALHAMBRA LEGACY, and THE FAERIE RING. The quilts in this chapter show the wide range of design possibilities from using the Pineapple block itself. You may want to study them for inspiration in developing your own borders.

When piecing complex color and shape variations, such as the ones in this chapter, the ability to write the color placement directly on the foundation is of immeasurable design help, avoiding time-consuming errors. Mistakes are difficult, if not impossible, to correct after a block is pieced, so a momentary lapse in concentration can be costly. Even on simple-appearing traditional quilts where the diagonal stars are different colors or fabrics, four adjoining blocks are involved to form one star. In such cases, each block may have up to four different diagonal colors, as in SPACE LIGHTS (page 113). Unfortunately, misplacement of the colors cannot be corrected just by turning the block unless the color arrangement and the design are symmetrical.

PINEAPPLE PROJECTS

Four updated versions of the traditional Pineapple will be explained in the following projects. Both those of you who are new to the Pineapple quilt and those who have had a long love-affair with the pattern will find quilts that will engage your imagination and have you reaching for fabric. The patterns may even lead you to create your own innovations. The projects range from classic designs to those with changes in color, strip size, and block configuration, taking us "back to the future." All were pieced by sewing machine.

Basic Pineapple

To familiarize yourself with the basics, try this 6" block (pattern on page 115). If you make four, you will have a small wall-hanging or a very stylish pillow to show for your efforts. For easy, quick precision, use under pressed-piecing (page 147).

Directions

1. Trace the block on tracing paper, lightweight interfacing, or fabric. For multiple copies, needle punch tracing paper. See Appendix (pages 147–150) for foundation choices, marking, and needle-punching directions. For a finished-block foundation, cut out the block on the final solid line. For a block with the seam allowance included, cut on the final dotted line.

2. Cut a 1½" center square, and strips of light and of dark values across the width of the fabric an ample 1" wide.

3. Pin the center square on the unmarked side of the foundation, positioning it within the center dashed lines. Following the under pressed-piecing instructions in the Appendix, page 147, piece a light strip on each side of the center square, piecing on opposite sides of the center to help maintain the square (Fig. 5–2a, page 116). Add two more strips on the remaining sides of the center square. You can either cut pieces the size of the line plus an ample ½"

Cut sizes:
center square 1½"
strips 1" wide

Solid lines: sewing lines
Dotted lines: fabric edge placement lines

6" finished-size basic Pineapple block

or use both ends of a strip of fabric, one pinned in place for each opposite strip, cutting to shape after they are sewn.

4. Trim the excess fabric from Row 1 on the diagonal dashed lines, which leaves a ¼" seam allowance (Fig. 5–2b). For the second row, piece four dark strips on the first diagonal lines (Fig. 5–2c). It is possible to stitch two pieces at a time, without removing the foundation from the sewing machine. If you pre-cut the strips, you can pin and stitch around an entire row once you reach the sixth row.

5. Continue piecing, trimming any excess fabric after the strips have been pressed open to provide an accurate edge for positioning the next strip. The horizontal and vertical rows will contain light strips. The diagonal rows are made with dark strips. Alternate four horizontal-vertical and four diagonal strips until the block is complete.

6. The final row of dark, the outside corners, can be made from either a strip cut 2½" x 16" or two 3½" squares cut on the diagonal. If the fabric you are using has a directional print, it

is better to use the first method to keep the integrity of the print throughout the block.

7. Press the block and baste the fabric to the foundation, either in the seam allowance or within the block if there is no allowance on the foundation. Trim excess fabric so there is a ¼" seam allowance.

The Pineapple lends itself to infinite variations. Whether you are thinking of a traditional design, a variation, or an innovative approach, the Pineapple Planning Sheet in Fig. 5–3 (page 117) may help you plan the color arrangement.

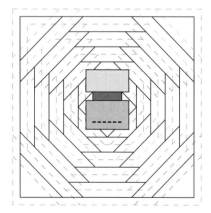

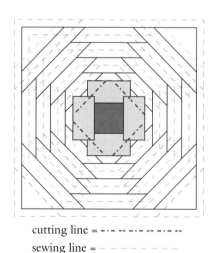

cutting line = – ·· – – ·· – – ·· –
sewing line = – – – – – – –

Fig. 5–2a. Piecing first strips on opposite sides of the center.

Fig. 5–2b. Row 1 complete, before trimming.

Fig. 5–2c. Row 2 complete, and trimmed.

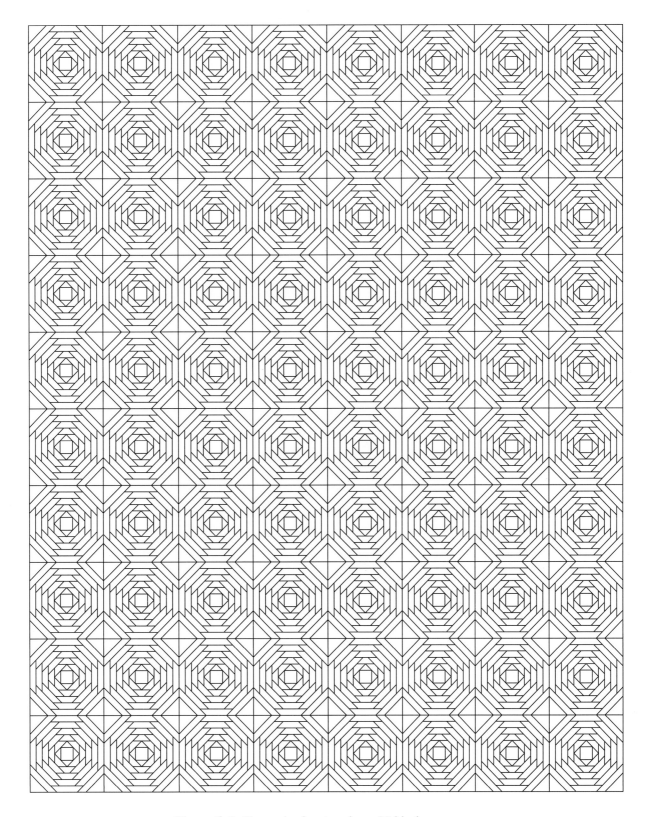

Figure 5–3. Pineapple planning sheet, 80 blocks.

You may copy this page for personal use only.

Berrypatch

Photo 5–15. BERRYPATCH, 32" x 32". Made by Jane Hall.

This innovative design is made with the classic block, but the traditional coloration has been changed. Basic figures are apparent: horizontal-vertical windmills, large stars formed by the corners of four blocks, and circles surrounding these stars. Study the quilt layout on page 120. In BERRYPATCH, analogous colors (colors next to each other on the color wheel) were used for the stars, running diagonally from upper left to lower right. The surrounding arcs of the horizontal and vertical planes have adjacent analogous tints and shades. The quilt was made with 10 hand-dyed fabrics, closely graduated in hue.

Because the quilt was designed around the stars, the built-in border made from background fabric was pieced into the Pineapple block at the outer edges of the quilt. A strip of the same background fabric was added, with a curved appliquéd vine framing the quilt. Finding a printed fabric for the vine, leaves, and binding containing all the colors of the hand-dyed fabrics was pure serendipity.

TECHNIQUE:
Under Pressed-Piecing

SIZE:
32" x 32"

BLOCKS:
Sixteen 6" (finished) blocks

BORDER:
4" (finished) cream print border with appliquéd vine and leaves

MATERIALS:
A run of colors – ½-yard cuts of 10 hand-dyed fabrics, bright red through dark navy blue

Background and border – 1 yard cream tone-on-tone print

Vine, leaves, and binding – 1 yard coordinating print

Backing – 1 yard coordinating print

Lightweight paper or interfacing for block foundations

Freezer paper for appliqué leaves

Batting

Usual sewing supplies

Optional: pre-printed block foundations (see Resource List, page 158)

Cutting Directions

BLOCKS

Number the fabrics from light to dark. Cut the fabrics into strips an ample 1" wide. You will not need to cut up all of fabrics 1, 2, 9, or 10.

Cut ample 1" strips of the cream print.

Cut sixteen 1½" squares for centers, following layout diagram for color (Fig. 5–4, page 120).

Cut a 2" strip of each fabric for block corners.

BORDERS

Cut four from cream print fabric 4½" x 33".

VINE

Cut four ¾" bias strips, each measuring 30", from the print fabric.

LEAVES

Trace the pattern (shown below) on the dull side of freezer paper. Cut out 32 leaves. Press each leaf on the wrong side of the print fabric and cut ³⁄₁₆" outside the paper.

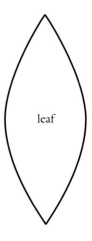

leaf

Full-sized leaf pattern

Construction

1. Prepare 16 foundations by tracing or needle punching (page 148) the basic Pineapple block on page 115. Code each foundation as follows: Number the blocks following the layout, and mark the planes with the designated color on each foundation. For this quilt, with the close variations in colors, each color was given a number rather than a name. To avoid mirror-image problems, take care to work from the same side of each foundation.

2. Piece the blocks, following the general Pineapple piecing directions in this chapter, beginning on page 114. Fabric should extend at least ¼" outside the edges of the foundations. Press, baste, and trim the outer edge of each block, with a ¼" seam allowance on all sides.

3. Lay out the blocks according to the quilt layout diagram and assemble the quilt top. Add the cream print border, mitering the corners. Remove foundations from the blocks.

4. Lightly draw a curved line for the vine on the cream border, as shown in the BERRY-PATCH layout on this page. Press the bias strips in thirds to make a ¼" vine and appliqué it on the curved line.

5. Fold under the seam allowance on the leaves, and appliqué them on either side of the vine, as shown. Remove the freezer paper.

6. Layer, baste, and quilt. (See Chapter 6, page 140 for quilting diagram.) Bind the raw edges with the vine fabric.

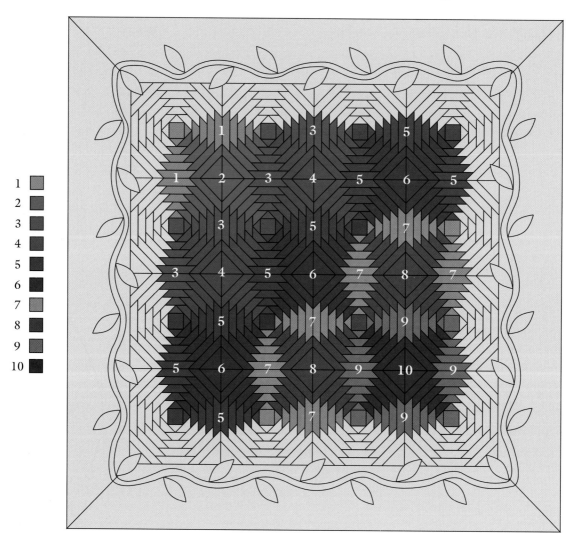

Fig. 5–4. BERRYPATCH layout.

Flying Geese Pineapple

Photo 5–16. FLYING GEESE PINEAPPLE, 40" x 40". Made by Jane Hall.

By lengthening the horizontal and vertical strips in a conventional Pineapple design, the diagonal strips become identical right-angle triangles, which create Flying Geese crossing the quilt on the diagonal planes. Appliquéd triangles extend the geese design into the border. This project is made with a tone-on-tone black fabric for the geese and 22 red same-value print fabrics, also used in the crazy-piecing for the borders.

TECHNIQUE:
Under Pressed-Piecing for blocks, Random Top Pressed-Piecing for borders

SIZE:
40" x 40"

BLOCKS:
Sixteen 7½" (finished) blocks

BORDERS:
⅜" (finished) inner black border
4½" (finished) outer red crazy-pieced border

MATERIALS:
Geese, centers, inner borders, binding – 1 yard black fabric

Horizontal and vertical strips and crazy-pieced borders – 3 to 4 yards total of assorted red fabrics (22 in sample)

Borders – 1 yard assorted red fabrics for crazy piecing

Backing – 1¼ yards red print

Foundations – Lightweight paper or interfacing for blocks and borders

Freezer paper, border triangles

Batting

Usual sewing supplies

Cutting Directions

BLACK FABRIC

1. Block centers: Cut sixteen 1¾" squares.
2. Border corners: Cut four 3" squares.
3. Geese: Cut ten 2¼" strips across the width of the fabric. Cut the strips into 160 2¼" squares, cutting each square in half on a diagonal, to make 320 triangles for the geese.
4. Border extension triangles: Cut a strip 1¾" wide.
5. Border corner squares on point: Cut four, from pattern on this page.
6. Inner borders: Cut four ⅞" x 31".

RED FABRICS

Cut 1¼" strips from each of the assorted red fabrics for the horizontal and vertical strips. You will need approximately 85" of red fabric for each block.

Construction

1. Prepare the following foundations:

   BLOCKS: Trace or needle punch 16 blocks (pattern on page 123; see the Appendix for needle punching, page 148).

   BORDERS: Four pieces of lightweight interfacing or tracing paper, 5" x 31", unmarked.

   CORNERS: Four pieces of lightweight interfacing or tracing paper, 5" x 5", unmarked.

   FREEZER PAPER: Cut 12 triangles for the border appliqué (shown below). Press onto the black strip, dovetailing the triangles, and allowing for a ¼" seam allowance on all sides.

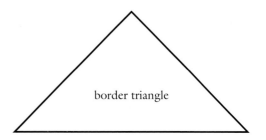

border triangle

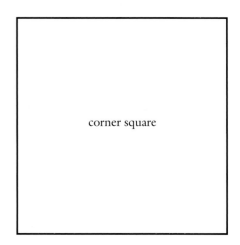

corner square

Full-size border appliqué patterns.

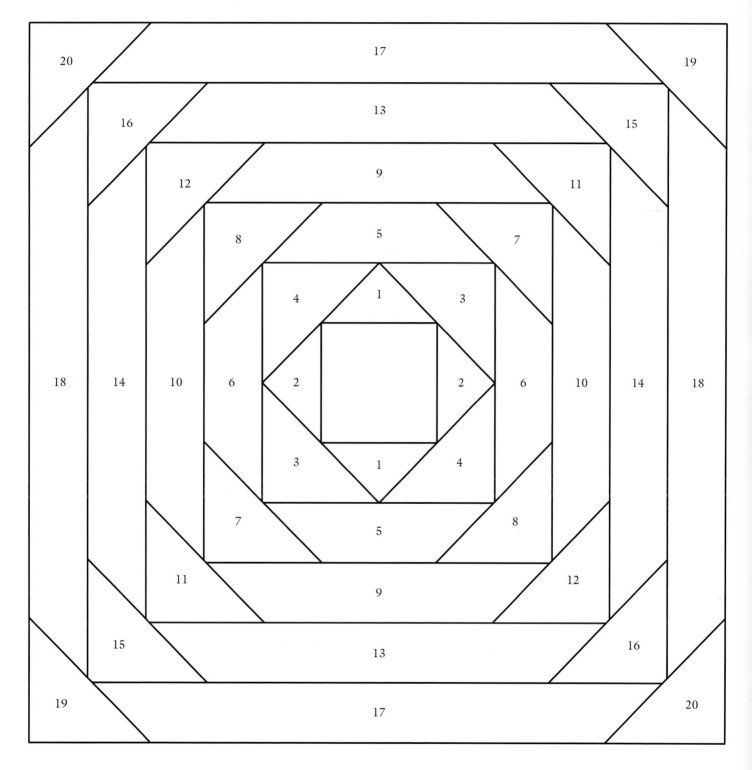

7½" finished-size FLYING GEESE PINEAPPLE block.

2. Select five red fabrics for the first block and use the same fabric for all four strips in each row. To be truly random, remove each set of five fabrics from the pile as they are used, until all fabrics have been used in a block. Mix up the order of fabrics as you begin the second round so no two blocks will be exactly alike.

3. Piece the blocks, following the directions for the Pineapple at the beginning of this chapter on page 114. Fabric should extend at least ¼" outside the edges of the foundations.

Press, baste loose fabric to the foundations, and trim the excess fabric to a ¼" seam allowance.

4. Arrange the completed blocks, making sure no blocks with the same fabric on the outer strips are next to each other. Sew the blocks together following Fig. 5–5.

5. Stitch the inner borders to quilt top, sewing on the outer edge of the block foundations. Miter each corner and press seam allowances toward the border. Measure and true the outer edge of the border.

6. Following the basic crazy-quilt directions (Chapter 3, page 54) construct four borders of red fabrics starting in the middle of each foundation. The corner blocks are string pieced on separate foundations. Place a black square on point in the center of a corner block foundation and string piece red strips around all sides to cover the foundation, following the random top pressed-piecing directions (page 145). Staystitch both the borders and the corner squares just outside the foundation edges, and trim any excess fabric to a ¼" seam allowance. Attach the borders and corners to the inner border, by using the previously-sewn inner-border seam as a guide.

7. The triangles formed at the junction of two blocks along the outer edges of the quilt were extended into the borders by hand-appliquéing half-square triangles on the pieced borders. Pin the prepared triangles in place, lining them up with the corresponding shapes in the blocks.

8. Remove the foundations from the blocks. The light-weight interfacing can be left in the border, if desired, for stability. Layer, baste, and quilt, by both hand and machine. (See page 141 for quilting diagram.) Bind the raw edges with a narrow black binding.

Figure 5–5. FLYING GEESE PINEAPPLE layout.

Glory

Photo 5–17. GLORY, 46" x 46". Made by Dixie Haywood.

This striking high-contrast quilt uses many fabrics of each color to add a subtle but interesting variation to the color fields. The block has modified corners that form stars when four blocks are joined. Notice in the photo, that the "sliced" Pineapple strips on the diagonal planes add a thin line of color that accents the stars. A white border is built into the pieced block, with a final string border framing the quilt.

This seemingly complicated design is, in fact, easily constructed. It is made of three differently colored Pineapple blocks, requiring attention in preparing the foundations as well as in piecing the patterns.

TECHNIQUE:
Under Pressed-Piecing

SIZE:
46" x 46"

BLOCKS:
Sixteen 9" (finished) blocks

BORDERS:
½" (finished) inner border
4½" x 46" (finished) string-
pieced outer border

MATERIALS:
Assorted red solids – 1½ yards
total

Assorted navy prints – 1½
yards total

Assorted white-on-white prints
– 1 yard total

Backing fabric – 1½ yards

Foundations – Lightweight
paper for block foundations

Freezer paper for border foundations

Batting

Usual sewing supplies

Optional: pre-printed block foundations, freezer paper with pre-printed grid lines for border foundations, template plastic for star shapes.

Cutting Directions

There are three widths of strips in the blocks: narrow red slices, medium white slices, and both blue and white full-width strips. It may be helpful to cut strips for the whole quilt at one time and label the different cuts.

For accurate piecing of the stars, make rough-cut templates for the two corner pieces. If you are unfamiliar with rough-cut templates, see Appendix, page 151, for details. Add a ⅜" seam allowance either when cutting the template or the fabric. Because it is easy to mis-cut asymmetric shapes and reverse mirror-images, make a test-cut sample.

RED ASSORTED PRINTS
Slices: ¾" wide strips

Stars: Cut thirty-six with template 2

Inner border: Cut two 1" x
36½" and two 1" x 37½" of
one print

Binding: 2" wide cut from
one red print

WHITE ASSORTED PRINTS
Slices: 1" wide

Logs for Blocks B and C: 1¼"
wide

Stars: Cut thirty-six with template 1

BLUE ASSORTED PRINTS
Cut sixteen 1½" center squares

Logs for all blocks and strips
for borders: 1¼" wide

Construction

1. Using the block pattern on page 128, prepare 16 foundations. (See Marking Foundations, page 148.) Refer to Fig. 5–6. You will need four of Block A (center blocks), four of Block B (corner blocks), and eight of Block C (side blocks). Trace the seam line for either the corner triangles or the star points, depending on the block. To avoid confusion, mark the colors on the unmarked side of the foundations on at least one each of blocks A, B, and C. If using pre-printed foundations, draw the center on point, and study the blocks to see where to mark the star line in the corners.

2. Prepare border foundations. Cut two pieces of freezer paper 4½" x 37" and two 4½" x 46". The foundations do not include seam allowances. Draw the sewing lines for the strings on one foundation, pin the four foundations in a stack, and needle punch the seam lines all at the same time (See Appendix, page 148, for tip on needle punching freezer paper.) The border strings can be any width you desire. The ones in the photo are ¾" wide to allow the use of leftover fabric from the quilt top.

3. Following the block diagrams (A, B, and C), use the basic Pineapple piecing instructions on page 114 to piece the blocks. On the sliced diagrams, sew the red strip first and then the white, using the dashed line as the sewing line for the red. Complete each red and white diagonal log before adding the next horizontal-vertical row.

4. When piecing the stars, trim the excess seam allowance of the white piece to ¼" after it is sewn in place to establish the placement line for the red piece.

Block A, center

Block B, corner

Block C, side

Fig. 5–6. GLORY is made of three different types of blocks.

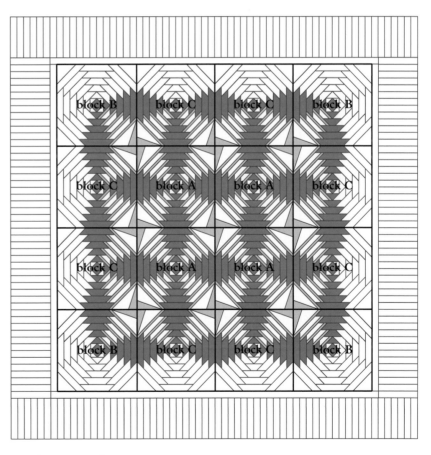

Fig. 5–7. GLORY layout.

5. String piece blue strips on the border foundations, with the fabric extending at least ¼" beyond the foundations on all edges. Trim the fabric edges to ¼" beyond the foundations. Staystitch along the outside edge in the seam allowance with a small stitch to prevent stretching when the foundation is removed.

6. Assemble the blocks according to the layout in Fig.

5–7. Attach the inner red border, butting the corners. True the edges of the quilt.

7. Add the string-pieced border, butting the corners in the same direction as those of the inner border.

8. Remove the foundations from the blocks and borders. Layer, baste, and quilt by machine. (See page 141 for quilting diagram.) Bind the raw edges with red.

whole pattern

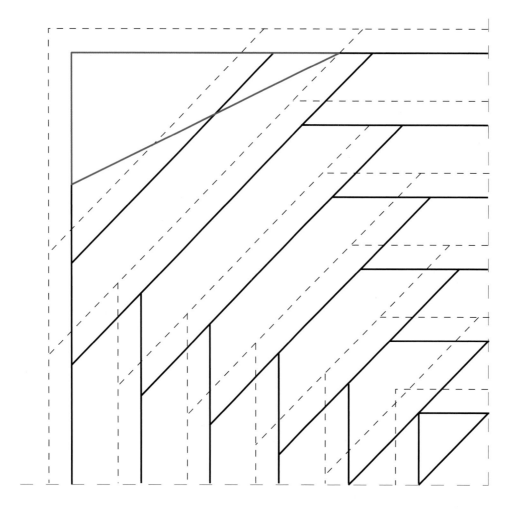

GLORY full-size ¼ block pattern. Use either the corner star lines or the log lines depending on the block being made.

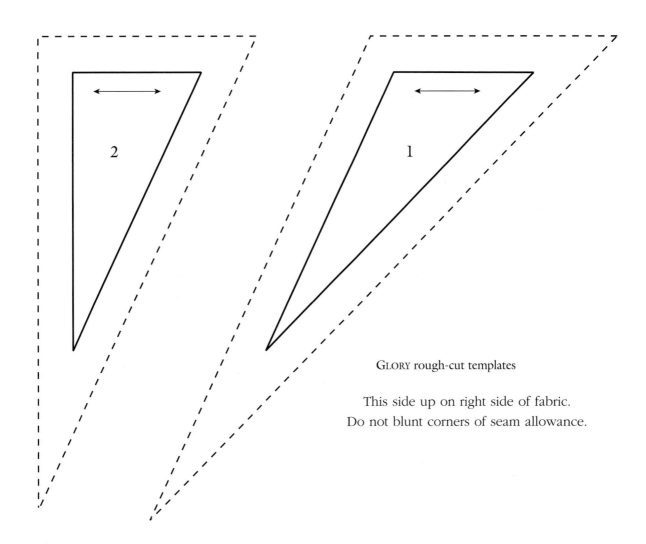

GLORY rough-cut templates

This side up on right side of fabric.
Do not blunt corners of seam allowance.

Block A

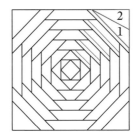

Block B

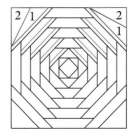

Block C

Shards

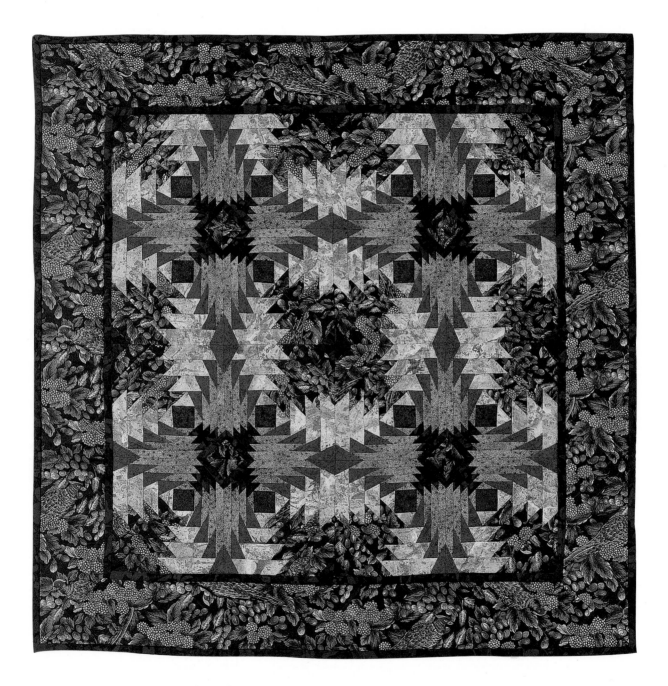

Photo 5–18. SHARDS, 28½" x 28½". Made by Jane Hall.

B y moving the center of a Pineapple pattern off-center, entirely new graphics are created in this already strong design. In this project, one set of diagonal strips remains parallel to each other, from one corner of the block to the other. The other set of diagonal strips is slanted, making "shattered" long-legged triangles that create a circular pattern when four blocks are joined together.

In addition to the color variable in each block, there is a size variation between planes in this pattern. In each block, one horizontal strip, one vertical strip, and one diagonal strip will be ¾" finished size. One of each will finish ⅜". The remaining two diagonals will be the "shards," each with the same-sized, long, right-angled triangle.

Photo 5–18

full quilt on page 130

TECHNIQUE:
Under Pressed-Piecing

SIZE:
28½" x 28½"

BLOCKS:
Sixteen 5½" (finished) blocks

BORDERS:
⅜" (finished) inner navy border
3" (finished) outer border of a large-scale print used in quilt body

MATERIALS:
1½ yards light-value fabric for horizontal and vertical strips. Can be the same or two different fabrics. (In the photo, the ⅜" strips are a light-medium value, and the ¾" strips a light value.)

1 yard medium/dark value print for the ¾" diagonal strips and outer border

¾ yard dark print for the ⅜" diagonal strips, inner border, and binding

⅓ yard "zinger" for the slanted triangular strips

Backing – 1 yard print

Foundations – Lightweight paper or interfacing

Batting

Usual sewing supplies

Cutting Directions

LIGHT FABRICS
1¼" wide for the ¾" finished strip horizontal and vertical planes

MEDIUM LIGHT FABRICS
1" (scant) wide for the ⅜" finished strip horizontal and vertical planes

MEDIUM/DARK FABRICS
1¼" wide for the ¾" finished strip diagonal planes

1½" strip for corner triangles (piece #34 on block pattern)

DARK FABRICS
1" (scant) for the ⅜" finished strip diagonal planes

2" strip for corner triangles (piece #33 on block pattern)

1¼" wide strips cut into 2" lengths for the "shards," a total of 160

Sixteen 1⅝" squares for the centers. In the sample, the fabric is the reverse side of the shards fabric.

Construction

1. Trace the pattern on page 133 and prepare 16 foundations. For the project, the pattern was printed on lightweight interfacing using an ink-jet printer. If this is not an option, trace or needle punch the pattern on lightweight paper or interfacing (see Appendix, page 148).

2. Mark the foundations with the colors you have chosen, taking care to keep the same side up for each block.

3. Piece the block following the basic Pineapple directions on page 114. The shard rectan-gles are not pre-cut into trian-gles, so it will be necessary to trim them to shape after stitch-ing each one. Because of the angles of the shards, it is not possible to stitch all four diago-nal pieces in a row without removing the foundation from the machine, although you may pin and stitch two at a time. Note that the corner triangles for the remaining two diagonal planes (the medium/dark and the dark fabrics) are cut from wider strips, and the fabrics are switched to accent the centers of the star shapes.

4. Press, baste, and trim the blocks with ¼" seam allow-ance on all sides. Assemble the quilt, taking care to rotate and arrange the blocks according to the layout (Fig. 5–8).

5. Sew the inner border to the quilt and miter the corners. True the edges of the quilt.

Attach the outer border, using the seam line of the inner border as a stitching guide.

6. Remove the foundations from the blocks. Layer, baste, and quilt by hand and by machine. (See quilting dia-gram on page 136). Bind the raw edges with the same fab-ric as the inner border.

Fig. 5–8. SHARDS layout.

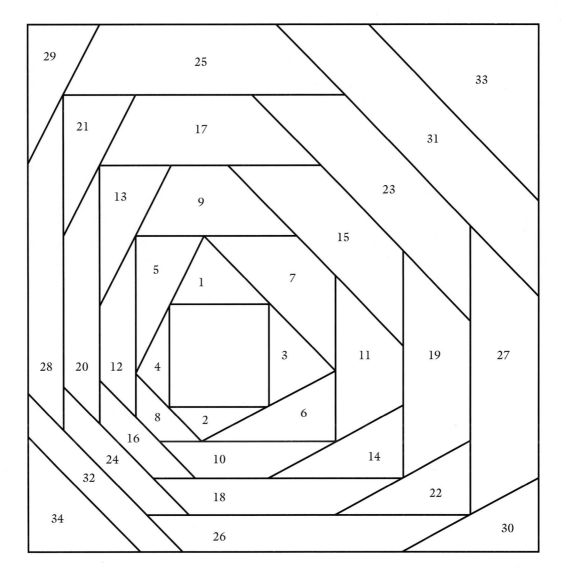

5½" finished-size SHARDS block.

Chapter 6
Quilting with Foundations

Most of the early foundation-based quilts, especially those made on permanent foundations, were not quilted. The foundations were generally made from waste fabric, often of differing weights. In addition to the weight of the foundation, the different weights and textures of the fabrics in the quilt top made quilting more difficult. The use of wool added even more bulk to be quilted through.

Silk quilts were often parlor quilts, made for show rather than utility, and they rarely contained batting. These quilts were most often tied, usually from the back. In the case of many of those made from fancy fabric, the ties were attached through the back only to the foundation and did not show on front of the quilt in order to present an unbroken pattern on the top. Many quilts in our categories being made today are still tied, especially the Victorian-style crazy quilts.

The popularity of machine quilting makes quilting through a permanent foundation easy, even with many cross seams. In some cases, retention of a permanent foundation may add stability that helps the machine quilting process. Interestingly, when sewing machines first appeared on the market, visible machine stitching was a status symbol, proving that the quilter could afford the expensive machine. Many were purchased on a co-op basis, with families each having their allotted time to sew with it. It was only later that machine quilting was considered second best to hand quilting. Happily, those days are over, and machine quilting has taken its place with hand quilting as a quilt art.

As well as filling a utilitarian function, quilting is a design element that can be addressed with either hand or machine work. Machine quilting, with its strong lines and ability to cover large areas quickly, appeals strongly to contemporary quilters. However, many quilters prefer to hand quilt, liking both the look and the process of hand quilting. The use of temporary foundations in these quilts with so many seams removes the extra layer of a permanent foundation that has inhibited many hand quilters. Fortunately, contemporary judgments are made not so much about what technique is used but on how well the chosen technique is executed.

The choice between hand quilting and machine quilting is just the beginning of possible decisions. It does not have to be an either-or proposition. Jane quilts many of her projects with both machine and hand quilting. She feels each technique has its strong points and likes to take the best from both. Ditch and outline quilting define designs, and the hard line of machine stitching serves that function very well. Hand quilting, with its softer gentler line, is used for curves and fill-in patterns. Areas with multiple seams close together are more easily sewn by machine, whereas large areas of plain fabric and curves lend themselves well to handwork.

The ULTIMATE PINEAPPLE (Photo 5–1, page 107) was machine quilted in the large diamond designs in each black windmill, and in-the-ditch quilting was used around the inner border. The diagonal logs and the border strings were ditch quilted by hand to make the many starts and stops less apparent. The curved designs in the large squares on-point were easily and effectively quilted by hand (Fig. 6–1).

Photo 5–1
detail

full quilt on page 107

Fig. 6–1. The ULTIMATE PINEAPPLE quilting design.

SHARDS (Photo 5–18, page 130) was quilted by machine in long swooping arcs within the narrow log areas and by hand in the shallow curves within the wide, light logs. All the ditch quilting around centers and borders was done by machine (Fig. 6–2).

Photo 5–18

full quilt on page 130

The selection of the stitch and the thread to be used is another opportunity for creative quilting. The "BigStitch," made popular by Jo Walters, is made with contrasting perle cotton thread and even stitches. It has much in common with Japanese sashiko. Other variations of a longer stitch and thicker thread can give a more casual and unsophisticated look. These have been called saddle stitch, fat thread, utility, and country quilting and have been used by

both current quilters and those of the past.

Both formal and casual types of the larger stitch are used by quilters who want a distinctive look that fits the style of their quilt, or just a faster way to hand quilt. Nancy Davison used it in her AMISH ABERRATION, made in a workshop taught by fellow guest artist Eileen Gudmundson (Photo 6–1). The quilting complements the embroidery she added to the border. She used several strands of embroidery floss for both the embellishments and the quilting.

Photo 6–1

full quilt on page 137

Metallic thread, used either for hand or machine quilting, can add an extra design element to plain or fancy patterns. The state of the art of these threads has vastly improved over the years, and they are fairly easy to use. CRAZY CRACKER (Photo 3–15,

Photo 3–15

full quilt on page 69

page 69) is quilted with silver metallic thread to accent both the ditch quilting in the crazy

Fig. 6–2. SHARDS quilting design.

Photo 6–1. AMISH ABERRATION, 41½" x 41½", 1998. Made by Nancy Davison.

★ Crazy piecing quilted in the ditch in blocks and borders.

Fig. 6–3. CRAZY CRACKER quilting design.

lenge, too interesting to pass up.

This idea applies first of all to string and crazy piecing. While embellished crazy quilts are still usually not quilted, non-embellished crazy piecing can be quilted with great effect. We often quilt both string and crazy piecing in the ditch to emphasize the texture of the piecing, as seen in REDCUBES (page 52), DESIGN FOR LIFE (page 52), and BORDEAUX STAR (page 16). Dixie sometimes also uses an overquilted design to act as a counterpoint to the piecing and to enhance the graphics of the quilt. CELEBRATION 2000! (Photo 3–10, page 53) contains both ditch quilting and overquilting in many of the larger patches of the border (Fig. 6–4).

Photo 3–10
detail

full quilt on page 53

piecing, and the curved and straight lines throughout the quilt. The quilting design for the entire piece is shown in Fig. 6–3.

When string, Log Cabin, and Pineapple quilts were quilted, it was often in the ditch. From a practical point of view, this avoided quilting through the bulk of the many seam allowances. In addition, quilters may have felt that the quilts did not require any additional design elements because the graphic quality of the pressed-piecing

was so prominent. They opted to use quilting merely to emphasize the pieced shapes and to hold the layers together.

Many quilters still feel this way. We believe they are wrong, that they have overlooked the way a quilting design can add another dimension of design and texture to the piecing pattern. With so many choices in quilting techniques and threads, the opportunity for creating special treatments for these four design categories is an exciting chal-

In the case of the Log Cabin and Pineapple quilts, with their regularly pieced logs and multiple seams, it is even more important to consider imaginative quilting lines that will reinforce the graphics of the designs. We have always quilted Pineapple designs nontraditionally to bring out what we saw in the quilts. It is possible to enhance one element while at the same time causing another to recede or even to form a new secondary focus.

Adding a quilting design that extends across the blocks of a quilt does not necessarily eliminate the need for quilting in the ditch. Ditch quilting can give important definition and stability to the piecing and the borders. It eliminates the distraction of floating seams that visually disrupt the flow of the design. It can keep a border from being skewed off line and can help equalize the amount of quilting across the quilt, avoiding the distortion caused when one area contains a focal point with more complex quilting.

Think of ditch quilting as the invisible skeleton of the quilt, with design quilting filling out the body. While machine quilters routinely quilt across seams, hand quilters often overestimate the difficulty of doing so. We feel the difficulty is more imagined than real. Yes, occasionally you may make a slightly longer stitch, and you may need to "stab" stitch at a particularly thick area. However, with a thin batting, and seam allowances trimmed and pressed open (see construction tips in the Appendix, page 153), crossing over the seams with a quilting design should not be an obstacle and is well worth the effort.

String, Log Cabin, and Pineapple quilts abound in linear elements. Color choices may change that focus, as can block size and shape variations. Curves, circles, stars, and diamonds are all easy to create from straight-edge elements and are common images in these quilts. Decide what components of the design to emphasize with quilting and whether the quilting should echo that element or provide a counterpoint to it. Above all, do not give the seam lines priority over the quilting designs.

The following examples show some of the quilting designs we have used for Pineapples. In NEBULA (Photo 5–3, page 108), Jane quilted triangular shapes in the diagonal planes of the stars, and the horizontal and vertical oval shapes were quilted in arcs, directed to enclose the stars (Fig. 6–5, page 140). The centers and corners were ditch quilted. The quilting was done both by hand and machine.

★ Crazy piecing quilted in the ditch in quartered circles.

Fig. 6–4. CELEBRATION 2000! quilting design.

Photo 5–3

full quilt on page 108

BERRYPATCH (Photo 5–15, page 118) was machine quilted in arcs around the colorwash stars, with corners and centers ditch quilted. The diagonal lines in the borders are hand quilted, as is the ditch quilting around the vine and leaves (Fig. 6–6).

Photo 5–15

full quilt on page 118

The FLYING GEESE PINEAPPLE project (Photo 5–16, page 121) has curved hand-quilted motifs in the red square-on-point shapes formed at the block junctures. The diagonal rows of black geese are ditch quilted by machine to enhance the shapes (Fig. 6–7).

Photo 5–16

full quilt on page 121

In GLORY (Photo 5–17, page 125), the piecing is overquilted with a design that forms stars as it is multiplied across the quilt. The strings in the border are quilted in the ditch (Fig. 6–8).

Photo 5–17

full quilt on page 125

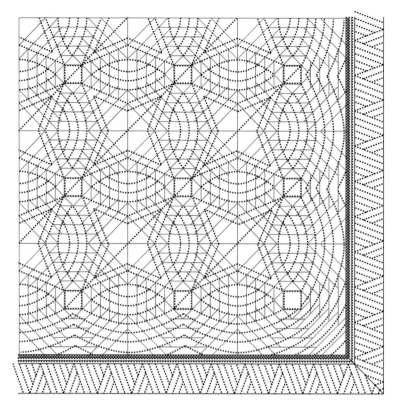

Fig. 6–5. CHROMA VI: NEBULA quilting design.

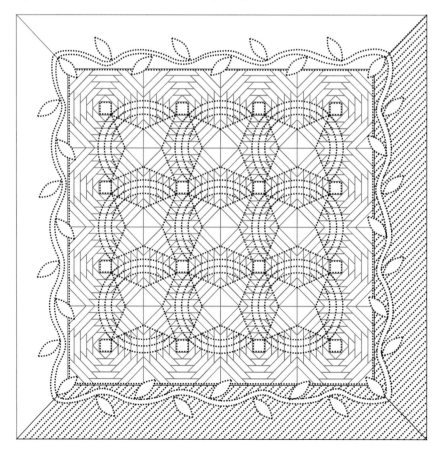

Fig. 6–6. BERRYPATCH quilting design.

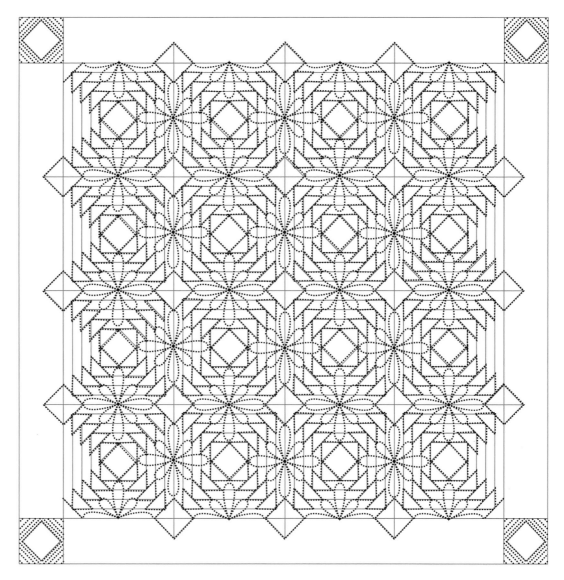

Fig. 6–7. FLYING GEESE PINEAPPLE quilting design.

Fig. 6–8. GLORY quilting design.

WEBSITE (Photo 5–13, page 112) combines ditch quilting in each seam with design-focused quilting. The horizontal and vertical planes are quilted with double-diamond lines that do not extend over the slices, to give the illusion the slices extend over the yellow strips. They in turn have a diagonal line across them, rotating around the star. The corners have a spiderweb-like design, and the center holds a small star design. The border quilting follows the design of the fabric (Fig. 6–9).

Photo 5–13

detail

full quilt on page 112

Think beyond the block and sketch out different quilting designs on a diagram of the quilt. For inspiration, look at photos of similar quilts and note how they were quilted. Lay tracing paper on the diagram so you can doodle freely without having to stop and erase your master sheet. We sometimes lay a large sheet of tracing paper on the quilt and plan and draw right there. This tracing gives both the size and scale of a suggested design. Jane sometimes has basted proposed quilting designs into a space, with long stitches and an unknotted thread. From a few feet away, this gives the effect of quilting lines and spaces. If you use a computer for design work, print out several copies of the quilt in outline or gray scale. With easily made copies, your brain is free to play with the possibilities.

We sometimes plan the entire quilting design in advance. At other times, we may know how we want to quilt only a section of the quilt, or that we will begin with simple quilting in the ditch. As we quilt an area, it suggests the next step. Seeing the quilting in one section usually makes the next decision seem clear and inevitable. This may seem to be a scary approach, but it has always worked for us. We believe it gives a better result than forcing the completion of a design before we are ready or becoming so paralyzed by indecision that we put off starting to quilt.

Decide, begin, and quilt on!

Fig. 6–9. WEBSITE quilting design.

Appendix

A foundation is a base on which fabric is pieced. The most common foundation technique is pressed-piecing, also termed "sew and flip" or "flip and sew." Traditionally, this process involves sewing two fabrics together on top of a foundation, stitching through all the layers and pressing open the top piece against the foundation. Succeeding pieces are added in the same fashion until the foundation is covered. Depending on the pattern, piecing can begin at an edge, a corner, or anywhere within the shape.

Foundations are also used as a base for appliqué in classic crazy quilting and to provide stability and precision for single shapes that will be joined to other shapes.

For the most part, the projects in this book use traditional pressed-piecing techniques, with added contemporary refinements. This appendix will detail both the basics and the fine points of this method. Specific instructions are found with the projects. We urge you to read this section first, so we are all speaking the same language.

HOW TO PRESS-PIECE

These three samples, using a basic string-piecing design, will show you the differences between the techniques commonly used for pressed-piecing. Each is simple, easy to make, and will give you a basis for choosing the best techniques for your project.

Random Top Pressed-Piecing is the traditional "flip and sew" technique. We most often use it for designs with random strips and shapes in which matching the points is not only unnecessary, but may not be desirable. This is the method of choice for crazy piecing and many string designs.

Figure 1 shows a random strip-pieced string block.

1. To make a 6" block, cut a 6" square foundation. The foundation will have no sewing lines drawn on it except for line a–b, dividing the block diagonally.

2. Cut fabric strips at least 1" wide. For a more interesting effect, cut differing widths, tapered at one end. Each strip must be long enough to extend at least ¼" beyond the foundation on both ends.

3. You can begin piecing anywhere within the lower-left section, below line a–b. Pin the first piece of fabric, right side up, on top of the foundation, making sure there is an ample seam allowance at both ends.

4. Position the second piece, right side down, on top of the first, matching one long edge. Stitch the length of the matched edges with a ¼" seam allowance, sewing through both fabrics and the foundation (Fig. 2).

5. Press open the just-added strip of fabric and pin it to the foundation (Fig. 3).

6. Add the next strip, placing right sides together, matching the cut edges of the previously sewn piece. Stitch, open, press, and pin as before.

7. When the lower section of the foundation is covered with fabric, begin piecing the top area. Lay a strip of fabric across the line a–b, right side down, covering the raw edges of the sewn strips (Fig. 4). Stitch, trim any excess fabric, open, press, and pin as before. Cover the top section with fabric strips.

8. When the foundation is covered with fabric, press the block on both sides and trim away any excess fabric on the outside edges to a ¼" seam allowance (Fig. 5). To stabilize the bias edges, staystitch with a short stitch just outside the outer line of the foundation.

Precise Top Pressed-Piecing is a method that gives a larger measure of precision. It involves pre-marking the foundation with fabric placement lines ¼" beyond each sewing line. It is, however, only as accurate as the ability of the stitcher to maintain a consistent ¼" seam allowance.

This is easiest to accomplish with either a ¼" presser foot or a ¼" mark on the throat plate of the machine.

The 6" pattern on page 146 is marked for both top pressed-piecing and under pressed-piecing. The solid lines are the sewing lines, and the dashed lines are the fabric placement lines for matching the cut edges of the strips. When you are top press-piecing, the sewing lines are covered by fabric and are not used as primary lines. However, on a transparent foundation, the sewing lines will enable you to check that your seam allowance is accurate.

1. Trace the block pattern on page 146, including the dashed lines.

2. Cut fabric strips the colors you want to use. Cut 1¼"-wide strips for pieces 1–9 and 1½"-wide strips for pieces 10–15. Lengths will be cut after the strips are stitched.

3. The numbers show the piecing order. Place the first strip on the foundation, right side up, with the long edges aligned with the dashed lines, having ample seam allowances at both ends. Position the second strip on top of the first, right sides together, matching the long edges. Beginning at one end, stitch through all layers from end to end, sewing ¼" from the dashed line. Trim the ends of the strips, leaving at least ¼" beyond the edges of the foundation. Cut the threads.

RANDOM TOP PRESSED-PIECING

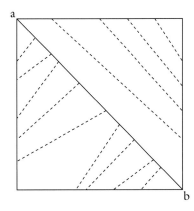

Example of a random top pressed-pieced block.
Dashed lines suggest possible seam lines.

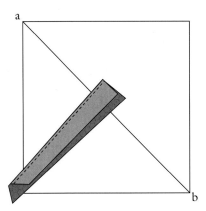

Step 1. Sew through both fabrics and the foundation with a ¼" seam allowance.

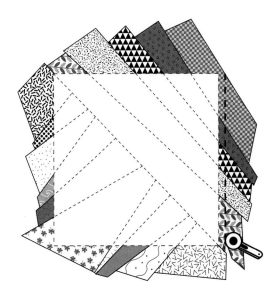

Step 3. First strip for top section.

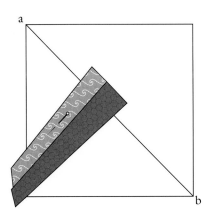

Step 2. Press open second strip and pin to foundation.

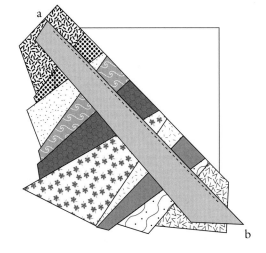

Step 4. Trim strings, leaving a ¼" seam allowance.

4. Open the fabric piece just sewn and press it against the foundation, anchoring it with a pin. Trim the ends as before. Ideally, for correct placement of the next piece, the fabric should be just short of the fabric placement line so the dashed line is visible. If the fabric extends beyond the line, trim it back. If it falls appreciably short of the line, you may need to remove and re-stitch the second piece.

5. Add the next strip, right side down, placing the long edge at the fabric placement line. Stitch, trim, press, and pin as before.

6. When the foundation has been covered with fabric, press the block firmly, and trim any excess fabric to a ¼" seam allowance beyond the foundation. Staystitch with a short stitch in the seam allowance around the outer edge of the foundation.

Any pattern can be configured for top press-piecing with the addition of fabric placement lines. Quilters who sew ¼ seams consistently often prefer this technique, which allows them to stitch directly on the fabric.

Under Pressed-Piecing involves placing the fabric on the underside of the foundation against the feed dogs and stitching on a sewing line on the top side of the foundation. While it may be confusing initially, it is quickly and easily mastered. This is the technique we use when we want the most precision. Extremely accurate block joinings, points and seam intersections are possible with this method, and it does not depend on the ability of the stitcher to adhere to a ¼" seam allowance.

1. Trace the 6" dual-purpose strings pattern (page 146) on a foundation, drawing all lines. The solid sewing lines are essential for this technique. The dashed fabric placement lines are helpful for positioning the strips.

2. Cut strips of your choice an ample 1¼" for pieces 1–9. Cut strips an ample 1½" for pieces 10–15.

6. Lay the first strip right side up on the unmarked side of the foundation, covering the solid lines by ¼". The cut edges of the strip should be just inside the fabric placement lines.

4. Position the second piece of fabric over the first, right sides together, matching the long edges. Pin through all layers, making sure the pin is placed well away from the sewing line.

5. Turn the foundation over. With the fabric against the feed dogs, stitch through all layers, sewing directly on the drawn solid line. Begin and end each line of stitching two to three stitches before and after the line.

6. Open the fabric strip just sewn and press it firmly against the foundation. Check that the cut edge covers the next sewing line with an adequate seam allowance. A scant ¼" is acceptable. If the strip extends beyond the fabric placement line, fold the foundation back on the next sewing line and trim the seam allowance to ¼".

7. Position the next strip right side down on top of the one just sewn. Pin, turn the foundation over, and stitch. Press, trim, and pin as before. Continue adding fabrics until the foundation is covered. Press the block on both sides. Staystitch the outer edges with a short stitch, and trim any excess fabric, leaving a ¼" seam allowance.

CHOOSING A FOUNDATION

Permanent foundations are made of such materials as fabric, interfacing, flannel, or batting. These are not removed after piecing and may affect the quilting process. In some wearables and wall quilts, the added weight can provide a sought-after stability. For hand-quilting or soft draping, the weight may not be desirable.

Foundations may also be temporary. Lightweight tear-away interfacing and papers such as vellum, tracing paper, freezer paper, and doctor's examining-table paper all are good temporary foundations. We usually do not use 20# bond typing paper

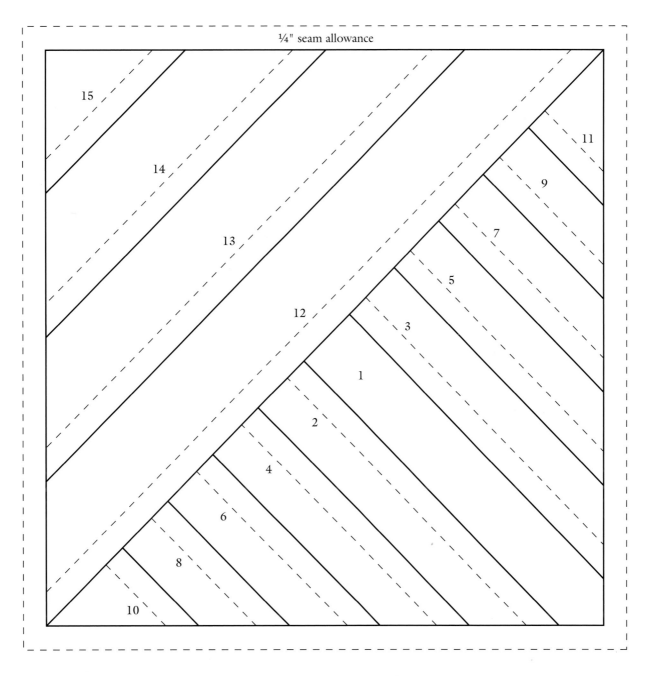

6" Dual-Purpose String Pattern. Dashes indicate strip placement for precise top pressed-piecing, and solid lines are seam lines for under pressed-piecing.

because we consider it to be too thick, causing stitch distortion when it is removed.

Foundations should be chosen depending on the project and its intended use. Whether you prefer to work by hand or machine is also a consideration. It is easier to work by machine on most temporary foundations, although some quilters do sew on them by hand. Permanent foundations, such as fabric and interfacing, are more easily hand sewn, and they add permanent stability to the piece. For a quick comparison of the advantages and disadvantages of the various foundation materials and marking techniques, see the Foundation Overview chart.

Freezer paper is excellent for designs with points and exact seams because it holds the fabric firmly. It is not very flexible however, and can be difficult to work with. Tracing paper is widely available and easily marked for multiple copies. Its translucency makes it easy to see the fabric and lines when under press-piecing. It tears easily, but often when least desired. Lightweight tearaway interfacing is translucent, pliable, and easy to work on. It can be kept as a permanent foundation to give body to the quilt and it is washable. However, it cannot be as easily marked as paper for multiple copies.

Foundations can be made with or without seam allowances included. Permanent foundations generally include allowances.

With the seam allowance as part of the foundation, the edges of the block are controlled, and there is little or no distortion, even with bias-cut pieces at the seam line. Another advantage is the ability to baste loose fabric pieces to the seam allowance at the outside edges.

Temporary foundations are often cut the size of the finished block, with the outside edge of the foundation used as the sewing line for joining blocks. Fabric must extend ¼" beyond the edge of the foundation for a seam allowance. This type of foundation avoids the difficult task of removing foundation material from the narrow seam allowances, especially when small fabric pieces have been sewn across the seam lines. The disadvantage is the possible instability and distortion at the edge of the block, which may make it more difficult to match seams when joining blocks. This problem can largely be controlled by staystitching with a short stitch in the seam allowance. In addition, on finished-size foundations, loose fabric at the edges of the block must be basted to the foundation inside the block for stability. Use a long stitch for easy removal later.

MARKING FOUNDATIONS

Except for random top pressed-piecing, patterns must be transferred to the foundations. The most time-honored

method of marking is tracing. Take care to use a sharp pencil, ideally a mechanical one, size .5 with HB lead. Place the ruler just off the lines being traced so the pencil re-creates the line placement exactly.

Fabric may be marked with a hot-iron transfer. Special pencils made for that purpose are used to trace patterns on paper. The tracing can then be used to make multiple copies when ironed on foundations.

Needle punching, long used for duplicating quilting designs, is a fast and efficient way to make identical copies. Pin the pattern on top of a stack of up to 12 sheets of tracing paper. Beginning in the middle, stitch on all the lines with an unthreaded sewing machine, making a perforated pattern. After sewing just a few lines, the stack of paper will adhere together and will not shift. When you have finished, check from the bottom of the stack that you have sewn all the lines before removing the pattern sheet. Each sheet has a rough punched side, which will help anchor the fabrics placed against it. Lightweight interfacing cannot be effectively needle punched because the holes are difficult to see.

Freezer paper can be needle punched, but the slippery side slides against the feed dogs, and the stack is difficult to control. A student gave us this wonderful tip: put a piece of muslin under the stack of freezer paper to be

FOUNDATION OVERVIEW

MATERIAL	BEST MARKING METHOD	ADVANTAGES	DISADVANTAGES
Permanent			
Fabric	Pencil, hot-iron transfer	Hand-piecing easy	Hand quilting difficult
Non-woven interfacing (Non-bias type only)	Pencil, hot-iron transfer, computer printer	Hand-piecing easy	Hand quilting difficult
Flannel	Pencil, hot-iron transfer	Can act as both foundation and filler	Hand quilting difficult
Batting, Fleece	Does not mark well	*Note:* Recommended only for string and crazy piecing Use with fabric backing	
Temporary			
Removable interfacing	Pencil, hot-iron transfer, computer printer	Lightweight; translucent; can be left in place	Cannot be needle punched
Tracing paper	Needle punch, pencil, computer printer	Lightweight; translucent	May tear prematurely
Examining table paper	Needle punch, pencil,	Lightweight; inexpensive	May tear prematurely
Freezer paper	Needle punch, pencil, computer printer	Stabilizes difficult fabric	Slips on feed-dogs
Letter weight paper	Needle punch, pencil, computer printer	Easily available	Weight can distort stitches when removed; not translucent

needle punched. With the fabric as a buffer between the slippery paper and the feed dogs, the stack will remain together and the marking will be accurate. Because there is no thread in the machine, the muslin will not be stitched to the papers.

Computers can be used to design blocks and to print foundations. Jane drew the block for SHARDS (page 130) on her computer and then printed it on lightweight tear-away interfacing with her ink jet printer. This method allowed her to use her favorite foundation material without having to hand trace each block. Both interfacing and freezer paper can be used in almost any computer printer; however, they must be used with a protective cover of typing paper in any heat-generating printer, such as a laser printer. Fabric ironed to freezer paper foundations can also be printed with a computer printer.

We strongly caution against the indiscriminate use of photocopy machines, tempting as it may be. Even the very good ones can distort copies, usually in one direction only. Machines may print accurately one time and distort the next. Digital copy machines, a bit more expensive to use, consistently produce accurate copies time after time. It is worth seeking them out.

MIRROR IMAGE

When fabric is positioned on the back of a foundation for under pressed-piecing, the design is reversed from the drawing on top of the foundation. If the drawing is symmetrical, the block will look the same. If the design or any part of it is asymmetrical, the pieced block will appear as a mirror image of the drawing in both line and color. This is a factor in several of the designs in this book.

If all the blocks are sewn with the fabric on the same side of each foundation, the mirror image may not matter because the total design will be reversed. However, if any of the foundations are inadvertently pieced on the wrong side, those blocks will be reversed and will not fit with the others. When foundations are printed or drawn on transparent paper, it is easy to become confused about which is the top side of the foundation. It is *extremely* important to mark foundations to indicate which is the stitching side and which is the fabric side. We mark with a word or a nonreversible number, which immediately indicates the correct side.

If a foundation is needle punched, it will have a rough side and a smooth side so it is easy to determine which side is up. If you want to have the block look exactly like the drawn pattern, you can cancel the mirror image by putting the fabric against the smooth side and stitching on the rough side. If the reversed image doesn't matter, stitch on the smooth side, with the rough side helping to hold the fabric.

DESIGNING WITH FOUNDATIONS

Foundations are a boon to quilt designers using innovative color or layout variations. The ability to write color, fabric placement, and construction sequence directly on the foundation makes piecing go more smoothly and prevents the frustration of misplaced fabrics. Whether piecing a traditional or innovative block, notations on the foundation can provide a road map to prevent time-consuming errors.

Recording the color and design areas on the marked side of the foundation, where the sewing lines are, is a common notation method. It will result in a design that is the mirror image of the drawing, with all parts reversed. This may or may not matter to you. To replicate the original drawing or cartoon without reversing it, mark the color placement on the side of the foundation where the fabric is positioned. Be aware that color placement can change a symmetrical design to an asymmetric one. Whichever method you use, it is essential to mark the color placement consistently on the same side of each foundation.

When Jane was preparing to make NEBULA (page 108), she marked all 64 blocks at one sitting, numbering and coloring them with the appropriate colored pencils. Although the individual blocks were colored asymmetrically, the finished quilt was symmetrical.

In SPACE LIGHTS (page 113), both the coloring of the individual blocks and the quilt itself were asymmetrical. Dixie composed the colors as the piecing proceeded and, to avoid confusion, marked the color placement on the fabric side of the blocks. Both of these marking schemes work. Just be consistent.

CUTTING FABRIC

Pressed-piecing with any of these techniques requires slightly oversized pieces of fabric for the patches. Part of this is caused by the process itself, with the fabric folded against the extra layer of a foundation, and part of it is the potential for mispositioning a patch. This can be caused by the width of the seam allowance, the size of the patch, or a carelessly cut or placed angle. Adding to the problem, quilters frequently off-set the line of their ruler slightly and cut strips slightly narrower than required. It is important to cover the next line of stitching with an adequate seam allowance. This may be a scant ¼", but should not be less than ⅛". Cutting fabric pieces slightly larger builds in a "fudge factor" for minor adjustments and will make all the difference in the world in the success of your foundation piecing. Use the following guidelines for cutting fabric for pressed-piecing:

Squares and Strips

Cut strips and squares an ample measurement, about 1/16" wider than normal.

Triangles

Cut triangles with a ⅜" seam allowance, rather than the usual ¼" seam allowance.

Half- and Quarter-Square Triangles

Triangles produced from squares should have approximately ⅜" seam allowance on all sides.

1. For half-square triangles, add 1⅜" to the finished measurement of the short side of a triangle to make a square that will be cut in half diagonally.
2. For quarter-square triangles, add 1¾" to the measurement of the long side of the triangle to make a square that will be cut on both diagonals.

All Other Shapes

Make a "rough-cut" template of the finished-sized shape on scrap paper and use it as a guide to cut fabric pieces with a ⅜" seam allowance. This method retains the proper grain and print line and, most importantly, provides an ample seam allowance and maintains the angles of the shape for accurate pressed-piecing. You can use freezer paper for a rough-cut template to prevent the template from slipping as you cut a stack of fabrics.

If the rough-cut template is an asymmetrical shape, you need to lay it on the correct side of the fabric when cutting so that the piece will fit properly on the appropriate side of the foundation. For example, if you are sewing on the drawn-side of the foundation, with the fabric underneath on the undrawn side, place the rough-cut template on the wrong side of the fabric. Conversely, if you are sewing with the fabric on top, the template should go on the right side of the fabric. Make a test cut to be sure the piece fits the space with the correct side of the fabric face up.

Exception

The first piece positioned on a pressed-piece block should be cut with a regular ¼" seam allowance. If it is cut too large, when the second piece is added, the seam allowance will be sewn too deep and the added piece will fall short of the next sewing line.

Focus Cutting

Normally, quilters take pains to cut fabric on the proper grain-line. Rough cutting is designed to help them do that, as well as to control print lines and directions. However, there are times to make exceptions to conventional cutting wisdom and use "focus cutting."

To focus cut a special motif from a fabric, use a template made of transparent paper or plastic. Cut the template the size of the patch, including ¼" seam allowances. Trace the outline of the fabric motif on the template. Align the template tracing on the fabric to cut the patch. Position the patch carefully on the foundation, perhaps using top pressed-piecing when sewing this piece for better control.

Focus-cutting will often put your patch off-grain. You may also want to cut pieces or strips of fabric off-grain to take advantage of motifs, stripes, or plaids. No matter how severe the bias cut may be or how stretchy the fabric, the block will be square and flat because foundations are stabilizing and forgiving.

Trimming

Oversized pieces will allow you to press-piece quickly and to amply cover the next space. However, they must be trimmed after the piece is pressed open and before adding the next piece. If the seam allowance is too wide, the next piece will be difficult to position accurately. If the edges are matched, the added piece will fall short of the space it is designed to cover. Fold the foundation back on the next sewing line and trim the excess fabric to a scant ¼" seam allowance. This gives an accurate edge on which to lay the next piece to be sewn. Trimming also reduces bulk in the block and makes it easier to quilt across seams.

One way to further reduce bulk is to grade the seams as you construct the block by placing

the top strip slightly away from the edge of the previously sewn piece. You can also pull the seam allowance away from the foundation and cut the edge of it at a slight angle. Either method can be used to avoid shadowing when a light and dark fabric are stitched together.

STITCHING
Stitch Length

Stitching can be done by hand or by machine, although foundation piecing is user-friendly even to novice machine users. For permanent foundations, use a normal stitch length. For temporary foundations, use a shorter than usual stitch: 14–16 per inch on machines made in the United States, 1.75 on a metric machine. These stitch sizes will hold the foundation assembly together securely and avoid distortion and loose stitches when the foundation is removed. This stitch length also makes it feasible to correct stitching errors relatively easily. Some pre-printed foundations are made of heavier paper. For these, it is necessary to use an even smaller stitch length, 20–22 per inch. If you should have to "unsew," take care not to tear the foundations.

You do not need to backstitch with most of the pressed-piecing techniques. Instead, begin and end each line of stitching two to three stitches before and after the line. These stitches will be crossed and anchored by

the next line of stitching.

Staystitching and Basting

On a finished-size foundation, use the same or shorter stitch length you used for piecing to staystitch the outer edges of a block in the seam allowance. On the other hand, use the longest basting stitch possible to anchor fabric temporarily to a foundation at the corners or outside edges to make removal easier.

Quick Sewing

Use quick-sewing techniques when possible, such as chain-piecing and assembly-line methods. It promotes accuracy and often saves time to sew identical blocks at the same time. For blocks that are pieced starting in the center, such as string blocks, Courthouse Steps, and Pineapples, you may be able to add two or more pieces to the foundations before you stop to press and trim.

PRESSING

When press-piecing, press firmly against the previous seam as each piece is added. Many fabrics can be finger pressed successfully as the piecing progresses. Some quilters like to use wooden or plastic "irons" to flatten the seams. Check to see that no pleat has been pressed in before sewing the next piece. A pleat cannot be corrected afterwards.

When a block with a temporary foundation is completed, it

is a good idea to press it on both sides. It is essential to do so on a permanent foundation to prevent bunching and puckering along the stitching lines.

Press seam allowances open when joining blocks to reduce bulk and to help the quilt lie flat. Pressing prevents distortion of points and seam intersections and allows easier, smoother quilting, whether by hand or by machine.

JOINING

Match the thread as closely as possible when joining blocks. When joining different values, use the least obtrusive color. Often, a medium gray is a suitable choice. You can also use one color on the top and another in the bobbin.

Use pins stabbed perpendicularly into the fabrics to match points and corners and to align seams. Fold the seam allowances open at the sewing line to double check that seam lines match. Pin the points and aligned seams securely before removing the stab pins. Some foundation materials are more slippery than others, so hold the pieces securely as you stitch.

REMOVING FOUNDATIONS

Resist the temptation to remove the foundation as soon as you have completed a block. You need both the outside sewing lines and the stability of the foundation for accurate construction of your project. On a large quilt in which the accumulated weight of the foundations makes handling difficult, you can remove foundations from the interior blocks after the surrounding blocks have been attached.

For easy removal of a foundation, crease or score the sewing line with a bodkin, large yarn needle, or crochet hook. Pull the loose pieces of foundation gently against a sewn line.

Some people dampen foundations to speed the removal process, but we have not felt it necessary to do so.

Leave the foundations in place until the quilt is ready to quilt. If there will be a delay between completing the top and quilting it, the foundation can help maintain the integrity of the piece. Do not leave paper foundations in place indefinitely because paper acidifies as it ages and can stain or weaken fabric.

Foundation piecing is a wonderful tool for your repertoire, allowing for precision and stability of piecing for everyone, beginner through expert. It by itself, however, does not guarantee piecing perfection. You must take care as always with marking, cutting, and sewing. The end result, even with a foundation, will only be as good as the care taken with the process. Properly done, it will result in extraordinary piecing.

Biographies of Contributing Artists

Nancy Davison, Pensacola, Florida, has been quilting for 43 years. Self-taught, she says "I did everything wrong at first, wandering through a long learning process with no input or criticism. Until Jean Ray Laury, I was re-inventing quilting all by myself." After sewing from childhood and with a background in building, drafting, and architectural planning, she found that quilting was a logical transition. Her quilts, whether made from traditional patterns or her original designs, have a flair that is all her own. She credits a class with Eileen Gudmundson for her AMISH ABERRATION design.

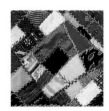

Photo 3–12

detail

full quilt on page 57

Caryl Bryer Fallert, Oswego, Illinois, is internationally known for her award-winning quilts, which are easily recognized by their luminous colors and illusions of light, depth, and motion. Her attention to detail has earned her a reputation for fine craftsmanship as well as stunning designs. Her CORONA II: SOLAR ECLIPSE was voted one of the 100 most important quilts of the twentieth century. Caryl's work has appeared in hundreds of exhibitions, and her pieces hang in museum, corporate, public, and private collections all over the world. She travels extensively and lectures and teaches to quilt and art groups internationally. Her goal as a workshop leader

is to help each student find the key to her or his personal creative style. She has authored articles and a book, and produces hand-dyed and hand-painted fabrics as well as patterns.

Photo 2–15

detail

full quilt on page 32

Lynn Graves, Chama, New Mexico, has been an avid quilter since 1985 when she was attacked by the "quilting bug." A clothing designer and maker, she began taking quilting classes and ultimately designed the Little Foot® as a result of her need to obtain an exact ¼" seam allowance. She has developed a series of patterns for traditional quilts made with paper foundations and printed with fabric placement lines to use with the Little Foot. Listening to her customers ask for a better "something or other" has led her to develop other items. She teaches year-round throughout the country, and can be found at major quilt conferences, surrounded by colorful quilts and enthusiastic quilters.

Photo 3–14

detail

full quilt on page 65

Eileen Gudmundson, Lillian, Alabama, has an art degree from San Diego State University in California and was a studio ceramic artist for 20 years before moving to Alabama in 1988 and rediscovering fiber art. Her ceramics were particularly influenced by the Korean Yi dynasty semi-matt black temmoku glazes and the black Seto ware of the Japanese Momoyama period. These interests have been transformed into her quilting, in which she primarily uses a black and gray palette. Eileen's first love in quilts are the Amish designs with their dark, subtle, and low-key color schemes. Her work has been published in the United States and in Japan.

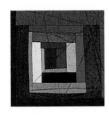

Photo 4–13

full quilt on page 86

Alice Allen Kolb, Fredericksburg, Texas, teaches a variety of machine decorative stitching, embellishment, and sashiko techniques at conferences throughout the U.S. and abroad. Alice has written articles for publications, including *American Quilter, Threads,* and numerous Bernina publications. She has written books on machine sashiko, crazy quilting, and a thread and needle resource. She has participated in the American Quilter's Society Fashion Show, both in production and as juror, and has designed garments for the Fairfield Fashion Show. Alice holds a M.S. degree in education, clothing, and textiles. In addition to stitching, she enjoys her family, the country life, and gardening.

Photo 3–13

full quilt on page 61

Barbara T. Kaempfer, Mettmenstetten, Switzerland, learned about quilting during a three-year stay in the U.S. in the early 1980s. Back in Switzerland, she began teaching basic quilting techniques, working with geometric patterns. In 1990, Barbara discovered the Twisted Log Cabin pattern, which attracted her for several years, as she explored the design in both quilts and in her book, *Log Cabin with a Twist*. She is now concentrating on using many kinds of fabrics, threads, and yarns and embellishing her quilts. Barbara has taught in Switzerland, Germany, Israel, and the U.S.

Photo 4–15

full quilt on page 93

Eileen Sullivan, Alpharetta, Georgia, has a degree in art education, and taught art in public schools for eight years. She began making traditional quilts in 1979 and started designing creatively in 1983. Eileen is primarily interested in innovative design and exploration of techniques. Her award-winning quilts have been exhibited throughout the country, and they are in several private and corporate collections. Her work has been published in quilt magazines and calendars, and she teaches and lectures across the country. She has created a line of floral and other original patterns with printed foundations.

Photo 4–16

full quilt on page 97

Kathlyn Sullivan, Raleigh, North Carolina, has her fingers in many quilt pies. A certified quilt appraiser and judge, she co-authored *North Carolina Quilts* and wrote the text for *Gatherings: America's Quilt Heritage.* Always a lover of antiques, she and Julie Powell together run Vintage Textiles and Tools. They specialize in old quilts, tops, ephemera, and needlework tools. She especially enjoys the design possibilities of Log Cabin quilts.

Photo 4–14

full quilt on page 89

Joan (Jo) Thrussel, Castletown, Isle of Man, British Isles, grew up on the island with a Methodist minister father and talented seamstress mother. Jo, a tomboy, was taught Manx patchwork, which was "simple enough for a reluctant sewer" by Nanny, her godmother's mother. She rediscovered Manx patchwork many years later after hearing a talk by Sue Hidson, who turned out to be Nanny's great-granddaughter. Sue gave Jo advice and help and inspired her to new levels. Jo demonstrates patchwork and quilting for the Manx National Heritage at Cregneish village, a restored historic site at the southern tip of the island. She was the prime coordinator for making a replica of an historic Log Cabin quilt, the Harry Kelly quilt, which was presented to the museum at Cregneish. The replica was made from old fabrics, and Jo's hand measurements, which were exactly the same as the original maker's, were used to make the strips.

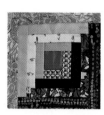

Photo 4–12

full quilt on page 78

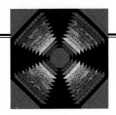

Bibliography

Brackman, Barbara. *Clues in the Calico.* McLean, VA: EPM Publications, Inc., 1989.

Fallert, Caryl Bryer. *Caryl Bryer Fallert: A Spectrum of Quilts 1983–1995.* Paducah, KY: American Quilter's Society, 1996.

Graves, Lynn. *The Frame Game.* Albuquerque, NM: Little Foot Press, 1994.

Hall, Jane and Dixie Haywood. *Perfect Pineapples.* Martinez, CA: C & T Publishing, 1989.

_____. *Precision Pieced Quilts Using the Foundation Method.* Radnor, PA: Chilton Book Co., 1992.

_____. *Firm Foundations.* Paducah, KY: American Quilter's Society, 1996.

Haywood, Dixie. *Crazy Quilting Patchwork.* New York: Dover Publications, Inc., 1986.

_____. *Quick-and-Easy Crazy Patchwork.* New York: Dover Publications, Inc., 1992.

Johannah, Barbara. *The Quick Quiltmaking Handbook.* Menlo Park, CA: Pride of the Forest Press, 1979.

_____. *Barbara Johanna's Crystal Piecing.* Radnor, PA: Chilton Book Co., 1993.

Kaempfer, Barbara T. *Log Cabin with a Twist.* Paducah, KY: American Quilter's Society, 1995.

Kolb, Alice Allen. *Crazy Quilt by Machine.* Aurora, IL: Bernina of America, Inc. 1997.

McMorris, Penny. *Crazy Quilts.* New York: E. P. Dutton. Inc., 1984.

Osler, Dorothy. *Traditional British Quilts.* London: B.T. Batsford Ltd., 1987.

Rae, Janet. *Quilts of the British Isles.* New York: E. P. Dutton. Inc., 1987.

Smith, Barbara, ed. *Pineapple Quilts: New Quilts from an Old Favorite.* Paducah, KY: American Quilter's Society, 1998.

The Quilters' Guild. *Quilt Treasures, The Quilters' Guild Heritage Search.* London: Deirdre McDonald Books, 1995.

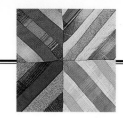

Resources

Bryerpatch Studio Internet Store
Caryl Bryer Fallert
www.bryerpatch.com

Hand-dyed fabrics in color graduations, "Flying Geese in a Curve" and other patterns, templates for under pressed-piecing

Georgia's Quilt Corner
Georgia Bonesteel
Portobello Marketplace
511 N. Main St.
Hendersonville, NC 28792
www.georgiabonesteel.com

Grid-Grip™ gridded freezer paper

Graphic Impressions
1090 Highpoint Dr.
Nicholasville, KY 40356

Easy-Tear™ removable foundation material, pattern stencils

Hall and Haywood
200 Transylvania Ave.
Raleigh, NC 27609

Perfect Pineapples (out of print, but available), foundation piecing papers for traditional and off-center Pineapple designs

Kolb, Alice
P.O. Box 946
Fredericksburg, TX 78624

Needlework publications and patterns, issued by Bernina of America, Inc.

Little Foot, Ltd.
Lynn Graves
P.O. Box 1027
Chama, NM 87520

Little Foot® for ¼" seams, paper foundations for precise top pressed-piecing, Pineapple design book, assorted quilting notions

Mekong River Textiles
Mekongtex@aol.com

Handwoven silk Ikat fabrics from southeast Asia

SCS Designs
Sonja Shogren
1815 Falls Church Rd.
Raleigh, NC 27609

Paper patterns for ultra-miniature Log Cabin and Pineapple designs

The Designer's Workshop
Eileen Sullivan
P.O. Box 1026
Duluth, GA 30096

Foundation pieced patterns for original designs

Through the Screen Door
PO Box 462
Kearney, NE 68848-0462

Variety of sectional foundation pieced patterns, including Tea and Chintz

Zippy Designs
RR1, Box 187M
Newport, VA 24128

Foundation Piecer, bi-monthly magazine

About the Authors

Jane Hall and Dixie Haywood are long-time friends whose shared fascination with the Pineapple Log Cabin design led to writing their first book together in 1989. Since then, they have collaborated on three more, this being the latest.

They both work with variations of traditional designs, using innovative approaches to shapes and colors. They are intrigued with foundation piecing in all its aspects and consider this old-made-new technique to be an essential tool in the repertoire of the contemporary quilter, as it has been for those in the past. While Jane and Dixie work independently on quilts with many types of designs, they each periodically gravitate back to the Pineapple with its strong graphics and infinite variations.

Jane has been quilting since the early '70s and is a certified teacher, judge, appraiser, and collector of quilts. She lives in Raleigh, North Carolina, with her husband, Bob, and Tilly the cat. She has six children and seven grandchildren. When she is not traveling and teaching, Jane is learning to use a digital camera so she can send pictures to friends of both quilts and kids more quickly and easily.

Dixie has been quilting since the late '60s and has been a teacher, lecturer, designer, and judge on the national scene since the publication of her first book on contemporary crazy quilting, in 1977. She lives in Pensacola, Florida, with her husband, Bob. They have two sons and a daughter, and three grandsons. In addition to quilting, Dixie enjoys swimming, cooking, and gardening, which mostly consists of keeping the jungle at bay!

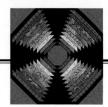

Other AQS Books

This is only a small selection of the books available from the American Quilter's Society. AQS books are known worldwide for timely topics, clear writing, beautiful color photos, and accurate illustrations and patterns. The following books are available from your local bookseller, quilt shop, or public library.

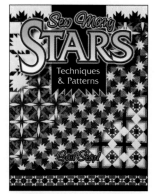

#5176 $24.95

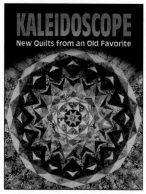

#5296 $16.95

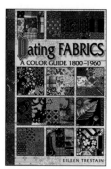

#4827 $24.95

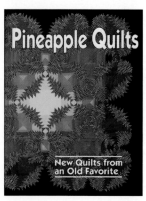

#5098 $16.95

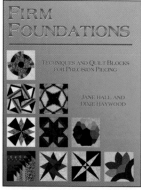

#4594 $18.95

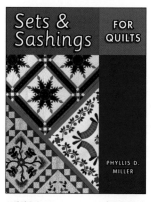

#5590 $24.95

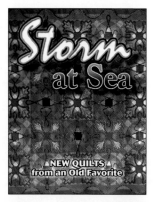

#5592 $19.95

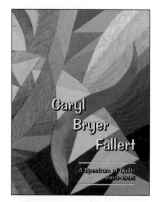

#4697 $24.95

#4995 $19.95

Look for these books nationally or call   1-800-626-5420